Minimalism & Decluttering: Goodbye Things, Hello Freedom

Discover Cutting Edge Methods to Declutter Your Mind and Live A More Fulfilled Life with Less (Beginner's Guide)

© Copyright 2019 - All rights reserved.

The following book is reproduced below with the goal of providing information that is as accurate and reliable as possible. Regardless, purchasing this book can be seen as consent to the fact that both the publisher and the author of this book are in no way experts on the topics discussed within and that any recommendations or suggestions that are made herein are for entertainment purposes only. Professionals should be consulted as needed prior to undertaking any of the action endorsed herein.

This declaration is deemed fair and valid by both the American Bar Association and the Committee of Publishers Association and is legally binding throughout the United States.

Furthermore, the transmission, duplication, or reproduction of any of the following work including specific information will be considered an illegal act irrespective of if it is done electronically or in print. This extends to creating a secondary or tertiary copy of the work or a recorded copy and is only allowed with the express written consent from the Publisher. All additional rights reserved.

The information in the following pages is broadly considered a truthful and accurate account of facts and as such, any inattention, use, or misuse of the information in question by the reader will render any resulting actions solely under their purview. There are no scenarios in which the publisher or the original author of this work can be in any fashion deemed liable for any hardship or damages that may befall them after undertaking information described herein.

Additionally, the information in the following pages is intended only for informational purposes and should thus be thought of as universal. As befitting its nature, it is presented without assurance regarding its prolonged validity or interim quality. Trademarks that are mentioned are done without written consent and can in no way be considered an endorsement from the trademark holder.

Table of Contents

INTRODUCTION	**5**
CHAPTER ONE - UNDERSTANDING MINIMALISM	**8**
What is Minimalism?	8
Minimalism vs. the Culture of Consumerism	9
8 Life-Altering Benefits of Minimalism	10
The Relationship between Minimalism and Decluttering	12
The Warning Signs Signaling Clutter that You Cannot Ignore	13
CHAPTER TWO - LAYING THE FOUNDATION FOR YOUR BEST MINIMALIST SELF	**16**
Powerful Principles to Help You See the World as a True Minimalist	16
Everyday Minimalist Habits to Get You In the Zone	24
CHAPTER THREE - DECLUTTER YOUR HOME 101	**30**
Light Decluttering: How do I start?	30
Tips to Maintain a Permanently Decluttered Home	31
Questions You Must Ask Yourself Before You Buy Anything	42
The 30-Day Wishlist Strategy	43
CHAPTER FOUR - FREE YOURSELF FROM EMOTIONAL AND MENTAL CLUTTER	**45**
Factors that Facilitate Mental Clutter	46
Must-Know Practices to Help You Deal with Mental Clutter	47
How to Identify Your Core Values	54
Everything You Need to Know About Decluttering Your Relationships	55
CHAPTER FIVE – THE SECRETS OF FINANCIAL MINIMALISM	**65**
How Minimalism Can Help You Financially	65
Minimalist Tips to Help You Achieve Financial Freedom	67
CHAPTER SIX - ADVANCED HOME DECLUTTERING	**71**

A Room-by-Room Decluttering Guide	71
Tips for Getting Rid of Sentimental Clutter	74
The Best Way to Decorate and Design a Minimalist Home	75

CHAPTER SEVEN - DIGITAL DECLUTTERING — 77

The Principles of Digital Minimalism	78
Important Advice for Defeating Digital Clutter	79

CHAPTER EIGHT - PERFECTING THE MINIMALISM EXPERIENCE — 8

Why We Need Experiences More Than Material Things	82
Experiences that are Better Than Any Material b ect You Can Buy	84
The Experiences that Make Far Better Gifts than Stufff	86

CONCLUSION — 0

INTRODUCTION

It can happen in the blink of an eye: one day you wake up and discover your life is clogged. You realize you don't really need most of the stuff you currently own. You discover you have slipped into the black hole of clutter and if care is not taken, you could slip even deeper and lose the true essence of your life. The possessions around your home could fall into any of these categories: things bought, things Inherited, and gifts received. At one point or another in your life, all these things served a particular purpose. You were happy with them, until you realized you no longer needed them. These items were tossed into a space of your home and began to occupy it permanently. Over time, stuff has accumulated and now you've lost control. It's like you are a protagonist in a horror movie and all these items have invaded your home with the sole aim of tormenting you.

You have picked up the right book. I can assure you of that. In these chapters, I will be exposing less-known ways of reclaiming your life, your mind, and your finances. It is one thing to notice the presence of clutter in your life, but it is another thing to know how to get rid of it. People tend to ignore the clutter in their lives, not because they are comfortable with it, but because they don't know how to relieve themselves of it. This can be the most frustrating of all. In fact, it is better not to discover the presence of clutter than to discover it and not know what to do about it. Truth is, clutter can easily become so large and towering that you can't help but notice it. These monsters of clutter are why I embarked on this journey. With my wealth of knowledge in your arsenal, you'll defeat clutter in no time.

I like to refer to myself as a "Declutter Agent." It may sound strange (you may be wondering, "Is that really a thing? Do people study that at school?") but we exist, believe me. People in modern day are finally willing to let go of the junk hoarded in their basements and attics, and experts like me help them achieve this aim. rom the young age of seven, I began what I fondly call "An xperiment on lutter." It is a work in progress, but I have discovered valuable information on how to starve clutter of their life force and hinder their growth. There is an antidote to this monster's bite

The antidote is this: minimalism and decluttering. The two go hand-in-hand and the wonders they work in your home and life are startlingly transformative.

In the ignorant mind, the word minimalism' can sometimes conjure visions of poverty, extreme frugality or even stinginess. This view is completely inaccurate. Minimalism puts you in control of your life. now how they say, "less is more"? Minimalism and its approach to decluttering will help you reclaim all personal spaces that have been eaten up by junk. Your home will finally become a place where you can live freely, unobstructed, and life will become more enjoyable and fulfilling, overall. It is possible to achieve this

The study of minimalism and decluttering is one that I have dedicated a great deal of my life and career to. And many of my past clients rave about the positive results they've seen after employing the methods taught in my seminars and webinars. Many of my clients have overcome depression and anxiety, and the majority have learned to regain control over their chaotic lives. These glowing testimonials have compelled me to compile an up-to-date and highly comprehensive archive of my methods. These are the same tools and techni ues I teach to my clients. People who adhere to my instructions rarely find themselves coming face-to-face with clutter again. All you need is the right dose of self-discipline and you are good to go.

The approach I bring to the topic of decluttering and minimalism is a simple and straightforward one. I understand that some of my readers will be first-time students of the topic, so it'll be best if it is watered down for their easy understanding. The act of decluttering can be mistaken as a se uence of actions that involve the process organizing or putting things in their right places, but I tell you there is more to it than that. The ultimate success of the process is dependent on mindset and a determination to maintain consistency. I will not only teach you how to declutter your home, I will also show you how to declutter your life, your mind and your thoughts. It is an all round process, and if one facet is ignored, then success might never be attained.

Think of the clutter in your life as an ever increasing monster. There is no stopping its growth. As time goes on, you will ac uire more household items, kitchen utensils, children toys and clothes. All these things will accumulate and pile into corners of the home. All of these might not appear dangerous in the real sense of danger, but clutter is a life poison, a virus that slows down the operating system of your life. nderstand that your home, mind, business and family are all at stake because of the presence of clutter.

A hinese proverb says that the best time to plant a tree is twenty years ago. The second best time is now. The solution isn't only in taking action, but in taking the necessary action OW o matter how stirred you may be by the points detailed in this book, you will never achieve tangible minimalism success until you begin to apply the methods listed. You'll feel a push while reading this book don't hold back. Draw out a small timetable for yourself and stick to it. Make a conscious effort to declutter your life. emember, only you can help you out.

CHAPTER ONE - UNDERSTANDING MINIMALISM

What is Minimalism?

The term 'minimalism' originated from an extreme form of abstract art that was first developed in the U.S in the early 1960s. This form of art depicted imagery that was stripped down to its barest so it could be more easily understood while passing across the intended message. The qualities of minimalist art were that they held a form of purified beauty for any beholder willing to look past their stripped down nature. In essence, the basic message that minimalist artists wanted to send was that there is always more in less. And as counter-intuitive as that sounded, the art form excelled and became popular with time. To help you understand its popularity, Alberto Giacometti's simple human-scale bronze sculpture of a pointing man sold for a whopping $141.3 million in May 2015.

The truth is that the concept of minimalism has been popular for centuries, even though many people have mistakenly assumed it to be a modern phenomenon. Minimalism has always been linked to pure, intentional art and design concepts. But it is also much more than that. Minimalism is about identifying the basics, the necessities, and sticking with them while eliminating all excess.

Our lives in this modern world are far from minimalist. Our society is constantly fed with the notion that the more you have, the more you are. Each day we are stuffed with more adverts and promos urging us to get this latest designer watch or those trendy new shoes. It's a cycle that never seems to end. A lot of us spend time chasing after these things, blinded and convinced they'll provide us with the happiness we need. I have been there and I can tell you that these shiny new objects do not give you the happiness they promise.

Here is my own simple definition of minimalism,

Minimalism is a form of intentional living that allows you to reassess your priorities and reconsider what truly brings value to your life. Minimalism strips you off distractions and allows you to reconnect with what brings you freedom.

As you read on, you may want to tweak this definition to better encapsulate your experience. Wants and needs vary from person to person. It's likely that minimalism achieves your needs in a different way.

Minimalism vs. the Culture of Consumerism

There's no way to sugarcoat it: we live in an obnoxiously consumerist culture. The pressure to consume is so strong that everywhere you look there's a new billboard shoving an attractive product in your face. ust walking outside can incite a battle of the mind and urges.

Being influenced by culture is normal, but some aspects of this culture can be quite damaging if care is not taken. Consumerism and minimalism are two opposing forces in modern day.The ultimate victor depends wholly on you. Every day, these large companies shell out millions of dollars in search of your attention. Social media influencers who act as their minions are also intent on getting you to consume more. The dominant message sent with these ads is, "You need to buy this product. Wealthy and attractive people all around the world use this product and don't you want to be like them?"

Advertisements are crafted daily with this intended message in mind. But ask yourself, "Did I need this before I saw the advertisement? Or do I only need it now that I know it exists? Is this need real or is a company trying to make me feel this way?" These are the basics of minimalism. It starts with the mind. It starts with talking to and cautioning yourself. No one is saying you should not be influenced by YouTube or Facebook ads, but learn to probe the intention of the sellers. What do they really want from you? Will this product offer value to you or does a company just want your money?

8 Life-Altering Benefits of Minimalism

There are many obvious benefits of decluttering, such as having a more organized home, but the benefits of minimalism go much deeper than that. Here are some of the biggest benefits of minimalism:

1. Emotional Stability and Clarity of Mind

The connection between the mind and the number of possessions we own is a strong one. Research has shown that a few minutes a day to clear out the trash, make the bed and deal with the laundry can massively impact our mental state and provide peace of mind. When we're not surrounded by mess, we subconsciously relax. When there aren't a million tiny objects to distract us, we can think more clearly and make better decisions.

2. Reduced Stress

Knowing that once you walk into your home, you'll find a pile of clothes on the bedroom floor, plates in the sink and books littered on the dining table is enough to make a lot of people fear the doorknob. It can create a psychological drain and if you're not careful with it, depression may even set in. Clutter eats up space in your home and can create a sense of claustrophobia, a feeling that your own home is being taken over. You must deal with clutter before it chases you out of your own home.

3. More Room for Things of Value

As I've illustrated, less is more. When you purge your life and flush out the things that aren't important, you are creating more space for things of value. As long as your life is filled with junk, there will never be space for what you really need. I don't just mean in terms of physical space, but also financially. If you're spending all your income on new clothes, how are you ever going to afford a comfortable new sofa? Call me crazy but I think it's much better to own three pairs of quality socks than a hundred torn ones.

4. etter Relationshi s

Minimalist principles apply to all aspects of our lives, and that includes our personal relationships. When we practice minimalism on a deep level, we become a magnet for better friendships and relationships. You see, even certain people in our lives can be considered 'excess.' How many of your friendships truly bring value to your life? Who are you only friends with because you want to seem more popular? Minimalism teaches us that having few but close connections is better than having many impersonal acquaintances.

5. m ro ed Time Management

Clutter kills time. Have you ever searched for a bunch of keys in a disorganized desk? No one wants to go through that on a busy morning. Clutter is a beast that can eat into your time. We waste a lot of time searching through needless junk for the items we really need. Think of how much time we'd save if we didn't have to endure this confusion!

6. a ier lanet

The earth is at the mercy of your minimalism. ess clutter in our homes means less waste in landfills and in the oceans. A lot of our clutter cannot be recycled. If we continue to purchase clutter, companies will only continue to produce it. And let's face it, we don't need most of these shiny objects. If you live a minimalist life, you can go on with a clearer conscience. You can rest easier knowing you are not contributing to the world's growing trash pile.

. Sense of ur ose

Motivation can return to your life after the process of decluttering. It is almost like you are starting life all over, like you have been reborn, giving yourself a second chance. Once you have gotten clutter out of the way, confusion leaves and a sense of clarity sets in. I have often heard people say that once they lose motivation or interest for a certain activity they stop for a while and clear their surroundings. There's nothing like the beauty that comes with the creation of space. It's a good way to remind yourself of the control you have over your life.

. **Emotional reedom**

Emotional freedom comes when we learn to let go of emotional clutter. We accumulate emotional clutter when we hold onto feelings such as malice, jealousy, grudges, and hatred. When you find the strength to settle scores, pay off debt and move on from mistakes, your mind is relieved. When we hold grudges or feel jealous of someone, this exhausts our emotional system. Imagine what you could have accomplished with that energy if you hadn't lost it to such negativity.

The Relationship between Minimalism and Decluttering

As I explained in my introduction, minimalism and decluttering are two capsules used together to cure the clutter disease. People use both words interchangeably thinking that they mean the same thing. This is an understandable mistake. Although they cover the same concepts, they are not the same. One serves as a springboard leading to the achievement of the other.

Decluttering is the beginning process for people who want to take back their lives and own their spaces. Some people who indulge in decluttering have no intention of living a minimalist life. For them it is just about decluttering today, waiting for the clutter to accumulate again, then decluttering again. For them decluttering is a form of therapy, a way to clean up their lives on a temporary note. As a whole, decluttering is hardly a life changing process. It is just like brushing your teeth every day or vacuuming the sitting room each morning. The result of decluttering is often never permanent. Most people often go back to decluttering every other month or year.

Minimalism and decluttering both share the same theme, which is the removal and disposal of excesses in one's life. Decluttering consists of a simple process while minimalism is an adopted lifestyle. Minimalism is a mindset where the practitioner has committed to only having things of value and importance in their lives. Minimalism helps to curb the excesses of consumerism so that decluttering will not be needed. It is all about living and surviving with less so that more intangible rewards can be attained.

The Warning Signs Signaling Clutter that You Cannot Ignore

Clutter is an ever-increasing monster, but the only problem with this monster is that you never notice its growth until the day it jumps out of the closet and grabs you by the neck. Just like a sickness, not everyone sees it coming. Study these signs and compare them with what's going on in your home right now.

1. **You're Overwhelmed in Your Own Personal Space and Private Life**

In my years of experience dealing with clutter, I can say that this is probably the most dangerous sign of all. It manifests itself in small ways. You wake up in the morning and remember all the appointments you have for the day and instantly begin to feel overwhelmed even before getting out of bed. Frustration sets in and the essence and joy of life is lost.

Once you get home, it seems like your own house has locked you out, even though you have the keys. You discover piles of confusing items that keep jeering their faces at you. You become confused and pray earnestly for the next morning so you can run away from the mess in your own home. Guess what? Clutter in the home is equal to clutter in the mind. Your home is yours and yours alone and you have to deal with it one way or another.

2. A istracted and nfocused Mind

All monsters are unattractive and they can easily cause distractions when they arrive. No one can remain calm in the presence of a gorilla-sized humanoid with horns and razor-sharp fangs. That is how it is with clutter as well; you can't get anything done in its presence because it causes one to feel scattered and unfocused. Even seemingly minor clutter like unwashed dishes can create anxiety and steal away focus. Clutter isn't only a hindrance to productivity, it can also get in the way of relaxation.

3. Buying to Impress

If you often feel tempted to buy particular items because you want to impress family and friends, even when you don't really like these products and may not need them, know that you are living a cluttered life. Chances are that most of the other things you own were bought with this mindset and are creating clutter in your home. Anytime you are forced to seek validation from an outside source other than yourself, the happiness you find will be shallow and never fulfilling.

. You Have Trouble Finding Things

Clutter swallows things up. When this happens, you'll have to beg this monster to release your things back to you. Have you ever wondered why you can't find the T.. remote, or your socks, or even a screwdriver when you actually need it? The answer is simple: clutter. These things have lost their rightful places in your home.

Books under the bed, spoons in the living room, knitting needles stuffed between the cushions: if any of this brings your home to mind, then you need to declutter. If you find yourself constantly misplacing things, then it's possible you own too much stuff. Once all extraneous items are cleared away, it immediately becomes easier to find items in the home.

5. **You Own a Junk Drawer**

Junk drawers are gradually becoming common in today's world, and this is a result of people having far too much stuff. The junk drawer is a dumping ground for miscellaneous items. Frankly, you do not need a junk drawer. If you can't find a home for certain possessions, then you should honestly rethink their necessity. As its name suggests, most of the objects placed in this drawer are junk.

6. **You're Ashamed of Your space**

Does the thought of a friend coming over to visit you send shivers down your spine? Do you start frantically cleaning and tidying when someone calls to say they are coming over for a brief visit? If you answered 'yes' to these questions, you likely have a big clutter problem. Let's get to work on it right away before clutter becomes the landlord and you become the tenant.

CHAPTER TWO - LAYING THE FOUNDATION FOR YOUR BEST MINIMALIST SELF

Powerful Principles to Help You See the World as a True Minimalist

To reap the full benefit of minimalism, you must be willing to pay the price mentally, psychologically and physically. As we've established in the previous chapter, minimalism doesn't just deal with the physical aspect of your life; minimalism goes deeper, penetrating one's mindset and attitude towards life. These following principles will help you prepare yourself for the journey ahead of you.

1. Your Possessions on't efine You

Contrary to what most people believe, you are not what you own. Your possessions do not define your worth and value. Unfortunately, many people make purchases with this misconception in mind. If you want to look good, go ahead, and if you want the latest accessories, go for it, but don't make these purchases with desperation. And do so without accumulating clutter.

It is not easy to practice minimalism in the world we live in today. We are constantly reminded of how we could and should be wealthier. We are bombarded by messages telling us the more we have, the more attractive, worthy, and interesting we are. But how many times have the products we've bought delivered on these promises? At the end of the day, we still have the same insecurities and the same obstacles. Chances are, even when you bought what you thought would be a quick-fix to something, you continued to encounter that problem. Your possessions will not fix what you're unhappy with. How much you own does not determine your worth. This may be a sign that you don't feel fulfilled in your life; once you chase what truly makes you happy, and allow yourself to be defined by your accomplishments, you will no longer need material objects.

2. **See your possessions for what they truly are**

It is time to take a bold step and honestly assess all your possessions. Look around your home and observe what's creating clutter. Ask yourself why you spent so much time and energy acquiring, maintaining and storing all these objects. The stuff we own can be divided into any of the following categories: functional objects, beautifying items, and sentimental things.

Functional objects get certain jobs done. They are needed to help us carry out everyday activities. Some of these are essential for our survival while others exist simply to make our lives better. It is important you understand that not everything you want is necessary for your survival. You might like to believe that, but it isn't the truth. Any functional objects that make day-to-day living easier are welcome in your new minimalist world. A home can function just fine in the absence of a skateboard but cannot do the same in the absence of cooking pots. Both things add value to a home, but the value of one outshines the other.

Beautifying items are brought into the home because they add aesthetic value to their surroundings. Art should be appreciated and embraced since this can sometimes add ambiance or a sense of calm to a room. But be careful as too many beautifying items can still form clutter, especially color clutter. Observe your shelf for a while and notice the presence of mismatched antiques. Just because you appreciated that sculpted object a few months after your mother's death does not mean that it should have a lifelong space in your home. We outgrow things and our love for them, and that is completely normal.

Things that do not fall into any of the previously mentioned categories usually turn out to have sentimental value. These can consist of gifts, inherited belongings, or objects that remind you of a particular point in your life. Sentimental objects remind you of the places you have been, the people you met along the way and the experiences you had.

When assessing your belongings, answer these questions:

- What value does this add to my home?
- Would I consider replacing this if it ever gets broken or lost, or would I be relieved it was finally out my hands?
- Did I need this item before I acquired it?

3. **The joy of simple living**

When you simplify your life, you are left with the basic, most necessary things that give you value and joy. Limit your purchases and acquisitions to the bare minimum so that you allow only what you need into your life. Having only the essentials in your home is a major component of minimalism. Doing so helps to prevent the influx of domestic waste (which is a form of clutter in itself). Strive to reduce your consumption rate so that you only have the things you need to satisfy your immediate needs.

Most consumers in our modern world can't even take comprehensive stock of the things they own because they own so much. Simple living helps you to stay aware of and responsible for your possessions. Perhaps you asked yourself one morning, "Where is my navy-blue polo shirt?" And even after weeks of searching you were unable to locate it. That is one major sign of clutter. You own things that you do not need or use and this has given birth to irresponsibility.

4. **Crave the availability of space**

Every once in a while, we just want to have a breath of fresh air. Have you ever tried doing that in a room full of other people? Of course not, because it brings no comfort. In fact, the room full of people is likely why you need that breath of fresh air. You'll find yourself breathing in cologne and body odor. It would be different if that space was clear. Naturally, we all feel calmer in an empty, clear space.

The absence of space causes distress. When there isn't enough of it, claustrophobia begins to eat you up. Many people believe their space problem can only be solved by moving to a larger house or compound. Within a few months of arrival, however, the clutter begins to form again on this new environment. Don't run away from your lack of space; tackle it head on and start creating more space. This is what minimalism helps you achieve. Every space becomes enough for you because you have mastered the art of creating more whenever you need it.

As I established in my introduction, clutter is a monster that eats up space. One day you wake up and discover that all the space you once enjoyed has disappeared and you wonder what happened. It was a gradual process and because space is silent, it uttered no word as it was being swallowed. Don't fret over your lost space. You might have lost it as fast as a finger snap but it is not lost forever. All you have to do is get rid of needless belongings.

You must take into consideration the amount of space you have in your home before buying more stuff. Remember that the space in your home is not emptiness. It brings its own aesthetic value. It allows all who live in that space to breathe easier and freer. Learn to crave this feeling, instead of stuff.

- **Less stuff means less stress**

People rarely consider this, but it takes a lot of physical and mental energy to manage all the stuff you own. After purchasing the item and that fleeting moment of what I call the 'buyer's high,' the fun of the situation begins to go steadily downhill. Not only does this item now take up space in your home, but you must expend energy keeping it in place and out of the way. And should the item break, it'll cost more money and time to have it repaired. Soon, it begins to feel like the products control your life, instead of the other way around.

The stress attached to accumulating possessions comes in stages. A sense of alienation and deprivation sets in once you discover that you don't own a particular item. "Gosh! I'm so out of style!" you might find yourself thinking. This is when stress begins to develop. There's a sense of feeling irrelevant if you don't own the right product. Then there is the stress related to acquiring the item. You start window shopping, surfing the web, and scrolling aimlessly through Amazon. Soon, you have an increased heart rate.

You realize you can't quite afford the item, but you put it out of your mind and buy it anyway. Your excitement outweighs your rational mind, but the stress seeps in once you click that 'confirm purchase' button. When the item arrives, you're filled with that familiar euphoria, but this doesn't last long. Once it loses its shine, it ends up in the same corner with all the other things you once loved, but that no longer interest you. It becomes another thing to throw out of the way when you can't find what you need.

Take a moment to remember life before you owned so many possessions. Everything was a whole lot simpler. You possessed that unadulterated joy of a minimalist, and probably more money, too.

I'm not trying to convince you to live in the woods, feeding on slugs and earthworms, with only a bed of hay and a wooden spoon. I'm only asking you to reflect. Imagine yourself without half of the possessions you currently own. Consider your life without your entire mug selection or the books you've owned for years but have never read. Consider your life if you only owned the handbags and purses you *actually* use. Chances are, your life is not any worse. And think of all the stress you'd be removing from your life!

6. **Contentment is powerful**

I can't stress this point enough: contentment is the foundation upon which a minimalist lifestyle is built. A greedy person or hoarder will never be able to practice minimalism to the fullest, unless they undergo a complete transformation. What's crazy about the modern world is that most of us *are* content with the things we already own – until we're harassed by the idea that something better exists and told we need to buy it now.

Once your basic needs as a human being are taken care of, then happiness should be in place. Your happiness should not be dependent on the things you own; when that happens, happiness becomes unattainable. When you learn to appreciate the little you have, you begin to see abundance in everything and life becomes even more enjoyable. Focus on what you have instead of what you don't have, because once you begin to compare your life with the lives of people around you, your hunger for more stuff never rests. Stuff cannot fill the void of your deep discontentment and dissatisfaction.

You must practice the art of believing that you have enough before you actually have enough. 'Enough' is, after all, a thing of the mind in the modern age when most of us have our basic needs satisfied very easily. It all has to do with self-control and self-discipline.

7. **Protect the flow of things into your life**

How easy is it for useless things to get into your life and settle there? Everyday more consumables pop up in search of a new home, and unless you practice self-awareness, your home is at risk of inviting this new clutter in. Protecting the flow of things into your life means you should only allow things of value in – the things that provide you with undiluted joy, free from the need to please or make others approve of you.

These clutter-building objects do not have legs or wings. We must ask ourselves, "How do they find their way into our homes?" Either we buy them or they are gifted to us.

Your home is your personal space; it is the only part of the whole world where you can be king or queen. A conscious effort must be made to protect the home from these unwanted materials. Before anything finds its way into your home, assess your entire situation.

The necessary questions here include:

- What role do I see this object playing, if any, in a few months' time?
- Is there a place in my life for this item right now?
- What is motivating me to purchase this?
- How long has it been since I purchased something that functions the same way?

You may be wondering, "But what do I do about gifts, giveaways, or freebies?" Politely refusing an item sometimes works fine, but most people don't have the mind to do that because of their relationship with the giver. If you truly feel you need to collect that item, go ahead, but make a mental note to take that item out of its place in a few months, and have it discarded, donated or sold. Don't allow this clutter to settle down in your home. Your home is not a dumpster.

8. **Live life free from the shackles of Possessions**

The best minimalists are those who have learned to manage the effects that possessions have on their well-being. The idea here is to loosen the grip that your belongings have on your identity. The emotional strongholds that we build around these objects can be binding and if we aren't careful, they may lead to suffering. Detaching from your belongings means finding emotional freedom, looking beyond the monetary value of possessions to see the real value of life.

The benefits of practicing detachment from possessions are numerous and life-altering. This will eventually lead to a less greedy personality. When you are no longer plagued by an insatiable hunger for stuff, you will find far more life satisfaction. You can finally find freedom from the material hang-ups of the modern world. Have you ever heard of families ruined by conflict over who gets to inherit a recently deceased loved-one's stuff? That doesn't have to be you!

Minimalism is a wakeup call to stop feeling defined by your belongings and to form attachments with aspects of life that create deeper joy. Help out in the community. There are new experiences beckoning to you. There are numerous people you can meet and forge new relationships with.

Although we might want to shy away from the topic of death, it will befall us all at some point. When your time comes, all the useless items you've become attached to will be left behind and serve no purpose. The things you leave behind will be what you're remembered for. While preparing for your minimalist life, take a few moments to sort through your belongings and consider what impression this will leave. This is not to make you fear or worry about death, but to make you understand that only a few things in your life are actually worth the space they occupy.

9. You don't have to own it to enjoy it

Consider this question: why do you have to own it to enjoy it? Adding a new object to your pile of clutter is not the only way you get to experience the benefits of that object. In this day and age, we are so eager to own things (and sometimes, even people) which we can call ours and *only* ours – but this is a silly way of living life. Items that are communal in some way are just as good. By borrowing or renting an item, you can still make good use of it without ever having to worry about its long-term place in your home. If you need a new book, why not borrow one from a friend or the library? If you need an outfit for a fancy event, there are many companies offering rentals of high-end clothing for short-term use. Rentals are much cheaper than purchases. Not only is this kinder to your wallet, it's also kinder to your home.

Everyday Minimalist Habits to Get You In the Zone

You probably knew this already, but minimalism isn't just a habit, it's also a lifestyle. For die-hard minimalists, it can even seem like a religion. For a little humor, consider clutter as the evil of this minimalist 'religion.' Just as every other religion has its everyday rituals to help followers stay connected to its teachings, minimalism also has its own routines and habits that serve a similar purpose.

There are simple habits that should be implemented daily or weekly into your new minimalist schedule. These habits may seem small but they'll create a world of difference. Most of these daily rituals can be carried out in mere seconds, without eating up too much of your time. Before we get into the habits of minimalism, let me explain a great strategy for integrating healthy new habits into your life.

- **A life hack for developing better habits**

When we try to create better habits, we tend to make things hard on ourselves. It doesn't have to be this way. Want to know a secret? You should find a way to attach the habits you want to develop to already existing habits. If listening to podcasts is part of your daily schedule, try doing this *while* doing something you don't enjoy as much. You could attach this habit to the less-enjoyable act of washing the dishes. Or you could connect the habit of getting ready for bed with the practice of clearing your desk space. When it comes to creating new habits, this is a tried-and-true way of making them stick.

MINIMALIST HABITS

1. Fire up your minimalist mindset every day

Start each day by reading or watching anything that has to do with minimalism. This way, you can ensure you always stay motivated. Refreshing your mindset about the powerful benefits of minimalism will help to keep you on track, especially on days you feel like giving up. Do it first thing in the morning because that is when your subconscious is most active and receptive to information.

Almost every ad on social media or TV is a promotion of consumerism. The more you pay attention to them the more you find yourself drifting away from minimalist teachings. Be diligent as you adopt this new lifestyle. Make a conscious effort to fill your morning, and in essence, your day with information that matters and information that will benefit you. Subscribe to minimalism channels on YouTube and follow minimalism influencers on Instagram. Start every day by revving your minimalist engine.

2. Find your tribe

The people you spend time with will inevitably influence your actions. You can't nurture a minimalist dream while hanging out with materialistic people. One party will influence the other, and I'll tell you now, materialism is far more catching than minimalism. No matter how disciplined you are as a minimalist, it will take a great deal of emotional and mental energy to not get sucked back into a world of consumerism.

If the people in your life live in alignment with minimalist teachings, it will be easier to make this new lifestyle stick for good. Minimalism will no longer be something you have to *try* to embody; it will simply be the new norm. You will not think otherwise. This is why it's important to find your tribe. This doesn't mean you can't socialize or get to know any other people (obviously!), it just means you need to be aware of who you surround yourself with and how that will impact your new life changes. Evaluate your life now and consider which people will be good and which ones will be bad for your promising new chapter. Come up with methods that will protect you from their materialistic ways if you ever need to hang out with each other.

- **ratitude**

Gratitude is powerful. Gratitude energizes the smile on your face and makes you the most attractive person in the room. This habit is easy to incorporate into your day, but as I've said, you will need a drastic change of mindset. The only difference between a grateful and ungrateful person is their mindset. Once you start looking at the world through the lens of gratitude, you instantly feel far happier.

Every morning, just before your kids or partner are awake, take out your special notebook or journal and list out three things you are grateful for. This can be anything! Your kid scored 80 on a pop quiz after you helped them study? Show gratitude for being blessed with a smart child. Is it a cold, wet, and miserable time of year? Show gratitude for having shelter from such terrible weather. Just think, you could be out there in the freezing cold right now! Contentment is only a thought away when you make gratitude a daily habit.

4. **Fill your life with e periences not stuff**

Value the experiences and memories that life brings your way. People will not remember you for the things you brought home from the mall, but for the experiences that you gave them while you were with them. Go somewhere fun. Go see a waterfall and experience the beauty. Cook someone a fantastic dinner. Shared memories and experiences are the rock on which friendships and relationships are built. People will always remember you for how you made them feel.

5. Learn to say no when necessary

Never underestimate the power of saying 'no.' Despite how small the word is, it carries a lot of weight and power. Lives have been changed and saved just because someone dared to say 'no.' As a minimalist, you have to cultivate the habit of saying no whenever it needs to be said. Saying no doesn't make you a mean person. In fact, it's saying yes when you shouldn't or when you don't mean it that makes you a coward. Do you find yourself unable to say no to people? Do these people always end up coming back? It's probably because they know they'll never be refused by you. Look around, some of the most respected members of society are those that say no at the right time. They are not easily swayed into other people's schedules and plans.

The habit of saying no can be learned with constant practice and over time. Saying no to others is saying yes to yourself and releasing yourself from future engagements and commitments which may turn out to be clutter in your schedule. Or worse, your bank account.

Say no to the kids who might want extra toys. Say no to friends who might want you to host a party even if you don't have the time and resources to do so. Say no even to your own self, when you mind is begging you to buy a new novel at the bookstore when there are a hundred in your home library that you haven't even opened.

. Plan a simple but nutritious meal

Simplifying your meals will teach your taste buds and overall palate to enjoy and accept the natural taste of food. The need to add extra flavoring to your meals will be reduced. This lifestyle change will prevent more packaging from finding its way into your home. A constant attempt to outdo yourself in the kitchen can be a drain on your time and energy. Have a meal plan that can be easily repeated with variety from time to time. Your shopping process will turn out to be much more streamlined and clutter will be far more controlled.

7. Employ space control mechanisms

Creating more space in your home is a decent way to deal with clutter, but it's not the best way. What you may have only succeeded in doing is providing more space for the growth of clutter. Instead of looking for how to create space in your home, employ mechanisms that will help you control the space that you already own. People have been building increasingly large homes and yet clutter still exists. Once we see the availability of space, it is our human nature to want to fill it up with stuff. For minimalism to take full effect, we must learn to suppress this urge.

Have two boxes placed at strategic points in your home. These boxes are for possessions that you are making up your mind to let go of. One of them will contain the things you want to sell or donate and the other will contain things that you want to discard. With that settled, stay alert and aware of what's eating up space in your home. Identify the things that have lost their value in your home and choose to either donate or discard them. This simple trick works wonders and clears up space within months of continuous practice.

8. Minimize your debt

Debt is a form of clutter on its own. It weighs you down both emotionally, financially and in your relationships with people. It may not work in exactly the same way as material clutter, but debt accumulated over time will always come with frustration, anger and depression. Minimalist philosophies stress the importance of preventing the creation of debt, but in the event that it has already happened, you must make plans to pay it all off and remove the burden.

Don't fret. It might seem like an insurmountable giant, but a step by step approach will nail it in the head. First, make up your mind to not accumulate more debt. Before you call your friends to ask for a loan or worse, buy something expensive on your credit card, consider deeply if it is necessary. Most times we fall into debt just because we're so convinced we'll get our act together later. If you can't do it now, why will later be any better?

Do some calculations and figure out what your weekly or monthly income is. From that sum you can set out a certain percentage for paying off debt, bit by bit. If you can make the payments automatic or a direct reduction from your paycheck, do it. It will also help to develop emergency funds; in other words, money you can fall back on when the time arises. Set up an account and send small chunks of your earnings into this account. Save money in this account over time and resist all urges to spend from it, unless you absolutely have no other choice and desperately need the money. No, your 'wants' do not count!

. Go for uality every single time

They say anything worth doing at all is worth doing well. I say, "Anything worth buying at all is worth buying in high quality." Substandard goods always turn out to be cheap because the sellers are sure that they won't last long in your possession. When we catch sight of these low prices, however, we find it hard to resist making the purchase. Inevitably, wear and tear occurs and you return to buy a new set of these same substandard products. Over time a growing pile of low-quality products appears in your home, when you could have just bought one high-quality product instead. Not only is this a waste of space, in the long run it's also a waste of money. Don't be fooled by that cheap price tag! uality comes with the extra cost and your peace of mind is worth that extra cost.

CHAPTER THREE - DECLUTTER YOUR HOME

Now it's time to get into the minimalist decluttering process in real detail. We have successfully established the foundations of minimalism, the importance of minimalism, and the habits that will set you on the right track towards a life of unrestricted freedom from material objects. This chapter will walk you through essential decluttering processes. Like everything we've demonstrated so far, it's vital that you make these practices part of your routine, and not just a one-time activity.

Light Decluttering: How do I start?
One of the most significant drawbacks of starting any new habit or task is figuring out where on earth to begin. When decluttering the home, there is always a place to start. When you look around your home and see clutter lying around your living room or your bedroom floor, something speaks to you and says: "You can't do this. It is too much. Where will you put all of this stuff?" Don't get worked up and overwhelmed by fear. All you need to do is adopt consistency. Decluttering doesn't happen in an instant. It is a process that takes time because it also took some time to build up. As you take time to practice it more and more, you begin to get better and better at it. Soon you find yourself naturally engaging in the process. It has become part of you.

The key to decluttering from scratch is to take everything out of its designated place. Turn the drawers upside down and pour out all its contents. Strip down the closet to bare hooks, rods, and shelving. Don't forget that you will need a free space to dump out the things to be either discarded or donated. I suggest you start with one small area at a time so that the room you are presently working on does not become crowded with materials and hinder free movement.

Pretend that you're starting life in your home all over again. Seeing belongings in a different place will change your perspective about its arrangement. And pouring out your stuff can help you identify some items that haven't been in their proper place for a while. Don't hesitate to take anything out of its designated space. Pick a portion of the house you are most comfortable with and start. There are many places you can begin decluttering, and no single one is better than the other. It can be your bedroom, or the attic or the basement. Just pick a spot. When you are there, you can look for a smaller portion of it and work on that: under the bed space, the wardrobe or the shoe rack. Don't neglect any part of it because every overlooked corner holds clutter that can grow if you don't pay attention.

Tips to Maintain a Permanently Decluttered Home

1. **hat stays and what goes** Once you have poured out clutter from its hiding place, you need to start the sorting process. This is the point at which you must find the root cause of all your clutter. The sorting process has three categories: Keep, Discard, and Donate. You will need three containers for each of these. Boxes will also work well to help you out, mostly, if you need to deal with smaller items. If you have a smaller box, you can use it for things that you have presently not made up your mind about. As you sort through, you will come across items that have you pausing and feeling confused about whether to throw them or keep them. Throw them into the box and go back to them later so they don't slow down your progress.

The possibility of you finishing up with boxes full of undecided materials is very high. You don't have to fret. Seal it up and place a date on it with a marker. Give the items some time and come back to sort through them again. By this time, you will have a clearer mind and judgment about the future of these belongings in your life. You should not get too entangled in the decision of having a box full of undecided items. That is a form of clutter on its own. Don't just dump it in the basement and forget it because you feel that you do not have the emotional stamina to let go of those things. The point here isn't to find a different storage place for these items, but to keep the decluttering process as fast and smooth as possible.

☐ **The discard box** The content of this box can be called the 'Discardables.' Don't linger on the name, as these items are basically trash. These items serve no purpose in your life. Don't get carried away and do not drop any of them into the 'Keep' box. The truth should always prevail in your decision-making. There are things you might feel still have value but inside of your heart you know they are trash; you just don't want to let them go because they hold certain memories or ideas about what you want to be. The discard box is filled with things that are hard to let go of. If it cannot be fixed, then you should let go of it.

Recycling some of these items is an option. Have your immediate environment in mind as you sort through these items. Go on YouTube and search for information about stuff that can easily be recycled for a greater purpose and value. Proper disposal of trash should be an important consideration as you sort through the pile. Where will these things end up? What can be repurposed and reused?

☐ **The eep Box** This will contain all the things that you want to keep. The possessions here will include everything that still brings value to your household and life, things you truly cherish, and things that are still functional and useful. If you haven't used some items in years then you should know that they don't belong in that box. They will be more useful in a donation box or in the box of undecided items.

☐ **The donation box** This box will contain items which are still useful but no longer serve any purpose for you. Examples are the expensive toys lying around the basement, despite your youngest child already being in high school. You can give them out to new parents. They will have more value in their home than it will have in yours. Don't feel bad about letting them go. You are giving yourself freedom, and you are providing those items with a new life where they will be more appreciated. Something will keep speaking to you saying, "But you might still need this someday." Resist the urge to succumb to that thought. If you don't need it today, the possibility that you will need some other day is very slim.

Be more generous with the items in your donation pile. Rest assured knowing that someone out there will appreciate them. You might also be worried about where to take your donations. There are numerous religious organizations that are always in need of materials to give out to the less privileged. The Red Cross and other medical organizations accept your donations to deliver in relief of IDP camps around the world. All you need to do is carry out a little research on the internet, and the right people will come knocking at your door to help you take out your donations.

If you are reluctant to release your belongings to the world this way, then consider selling them instead. The cash will provide you with more value than the item lying around the house. Hold a garage or yard sale. You will be amazed by the amount of money you can make from one. There are a variety of things you can sell, from books to CDs, DVDs to golfing equipment. You will be shocked by how many people in your vicinity desperately need the stuff you have been hoarding.

2. A purpose for each item: It is very easy for the 'Keep' box to become flooded with items. Before any item should be taken back into your home and life, it is necessary that you reassess its true importance in your life. Ask yourself the essential question about each item you come across. Each item in your 'Keep' box should be making a noticeable positive contribution to your life. Everything else should not go in this box.

While you're going through these objects, you'll come across many things that serve exactly the same purpose. They may have different decoration or packaging, but they ultimately do the same thing. This is a case of duplication, and it should be appropriately handled and taken care of. Minimalism is about clearing excess from your life. Some of these items in the home can easily multiply and clog up drawers. Examples are pens, paper clips, or buttons. Save a reasonable quantity and do away with the rest of them.

Other items that aren't in the class of duplicated items should now be scrutinized. Probe the essence of each item, figuring out its value and how much that value is needed in your home.

The answers that come to your mind will guide you on where to place the items, either in a donation box or in a 'Keep' box. Some items might have some form of value, but the space they will provide once they are taken out of the way might be more valuable. Provide yourself with that new space and get that object out of the way.

While sorting through and making categorizations, you could consider having an objective and responsible friend who is also a minimalist around you. Their presence will provide you with enough drive to do the right thing. Having to explain why you want to keep one stupid item or the other can be embarrassing. You will look through your belongings with clearer eyes and understand why you need to let go of them.

While going through your stuff, keep in mind that you only make use of 30% or less of the things you own every month. And the difference is hardly ever noticed. Some of the things you hoard and protect so dearly will serve no purpose in your life throughout the year. But because there is space, you just decide to house them. Be more rigid during your sorting process. Look for the essentials that make up the less-than-30% and keep them. These are your most important possessions.

3. A home for everything: In your own home, each of your possessions should have their own homes - space they will occupy from now on. It should be at the core of your minimalist mindset: everything should have its place. It is an important principle of minimalism. It's much easier for you to keep stock and prevent stray items from moving into your home when there are designated places for everything. When this is in place, it is easier for you to identify things that should not be in your home and things that don't belong in your environment.

There are considerations to be made while making these designations, some of which include frequency of usage, size, fragility, and proximity. The house is already broken down into smaller units of rooms. Sometimes, if one is lucky or rich enough, the various rooms are broken down into smaller compartments or spaces to contain some special class of possessions or items. For example, cupboards in the kitchen can hold ceramics and cooking utensils, and walk-in-closets in the room can hold all clothes. An item's home should generally be closest to the place where it is most needed. If you have any clothes lying in a pile on your bathroom floor, it's time to move them to the place where they are needed.

The things you use most frequently are to be kept closest to you in a place where you can easily reach them. You will want to be able to access these items without unnecessarily scavenging and rummaging through your other stuff.

Once you have identified and designated a place for everything, it will help to label each of these places so that anyone coming into your home will know exactly where to put things after using them. Use it as a sort of address for each item. Even your kids will get used to it and follow this simple instruction. Get your family members actively involved in the decluttering process. If everyone has a mindset of decluttering and minimalism, it will be easier to tackle this monster. A collaborative effort does wonders. Clothes should be hung instead of piled on boxes or chairs. Take the utensils back to their hanging spaces instead of leaving them on the kitchen counter. Return books back to the shelf instead of leaving them on floors or chairs.

Once you come into a room, try to find items that aren't in their places and return them home. It will only take you a few minutes out of the hours of the day and the huge difference will be noticed in your household.

4. Keep clear surfaces - Wide and flat surfaces are major breeding grounds for clutter. Most items will end up on clear surfaces, there's no doubt about it. Take a look around your house. Surfaces like the dining table, kitchen counters or living room coffee table are likely loaded with clutter. This will build up gradually until the whole surface has been colonized by junk.

Clear surfaces add a certain kind of beauty to any environment that surrounds them. They offer endless possibilities. The clear surface in the kitchen will help you prepare a quick meal without any hindrance. A decluttered dining table will accommodate members of a family for breakfast. The importance of clear surfaces cannot be overemphasized. We don't realize the value of a clear surface until we find one covered in clutter. Suddenly, we can't put a single plate down, or we have nowhere to put our laptop down for work.

To ensure your surfaces stay clear, you must adopt a new attitude and observe some basic decluttering principles. Your surfaces should not be used as storage spaces. By all means necessary, your surfaces should be kept clean and clear at all times. These steps will help you:

i. Clear off every single object on that flat surface. Whether they should be on the surface or not is irrelevant at this early stage. They will be returned later, if they belong here.
ii. Once the surface is clear, stand back from it and notice the calm that comes with having a clear surface. See how inviting the surface is, observe the beauty of space.
iii. Identify what purpose that surface serves in your home. Is it a surface that serves a specific function (such as a kitchen counter) or is it used during moments of creativity? Maybe you want to use it for something totally different from its former purpose. Once you have successfully identified its function, you can now determine what will be going back on the surface and what shouldn't be on the surface.
iv. Try not to allow more than three objects on any table. Anything more than that will constitute as clutter. If it's an essential object, put it on a shelf or anywhere else closeby. Allow surfaces to remain as clear as possible until the habit sticks.
v. You can add up to two additional items for aesthetic value on these surfaces. These will serve to complement the surface and keep it from looking too bare or boring.

It is one thing to achieve a clear surface and it is another thing to keep it cleared. A lot of people clear up surfaces every day, but before the day is over they are back to square one. These tips will help you keep your surfaces cleared for a longer period of time.

- **Drop your items on the floor when you get home.** It is a basic instinct to drop things that come with you into a room on a clean and clear surface. It is relaxing to get the weight off your hands and onto a clear table or counter. Then they sit there for hours or days, neglected because they are not in your way. The most important rule is to get nothing on the surface in the first place, place those items on the floor and once they make you trip twice, you'll be eager to finally put them in their designated place. It might seem too extreme for you, but minimalism has to be extreme sometimes, especially if you are a person that easily gets comfortable with clutter. Discipline yourself against clutter. With time, you will notice an attitude shift that has you organizing anything you come home with at all times.

- **Wipe surfaces down at least twice every week.** Wiping surfaces down draws your attention to the clutter growing on them. As you wipe, put away whatever shouldn't be on the surface and move aside anything that gets in the way of your cleaning. Discard any trash or useless pieces of junk and return the surface back to its initial glory. Do this at least twice every week.

- **Leave nothing for later.** When you're in the process of clearing things away, it can be tempting to tell yourself you'll finish off certain tasks later. Don't do this. If you're done folding the clothes, send them over to the closet immediately. Don't leave them on the ironing table. You were reading a book at the dining table when you realized you had to pick the kids up from school. Send that book over to the shelf before you leave the house. This is a major key to leaving surfaces as clear as they should be. Adopt the habit of putting things away as soon as you are done with them. Once you get used to this, the house can almost clear itself.

- **Prevent the accumulation of small clutter.** We are all guilty of letting 'small clutter' build up in our homes. You notice it growing but you never quite recognize it as clutter until one eye-opening day. As the name suggests, small clutter consists of smaller items, such as pens, paperclips, or useless little knick-knacks. It takes a while for us to admit this is clutter because the objects are so small in size. It's only when they build into a pile or they continually get in our way that we begin to admit the obvious: it's clutter just like most of everything else.

- **Finally, don't ignore the largest surface in your home**: the floor. It's so large that we rarely notice if there's clutter on it. It can easily get nudged away to the side and we forget that clutter is there at all, especially since it's at our feet. Don't allow yourself to neglect the floor in your home. Soon your floor will be hidden under clutter and you will struggle just to go from the kitchen to the bathroom. This can kill enthusiasm and productivity. Reserve the ground for the rug, your feet and the furniture. Remove all other objects!

5. Use small units of organization   Your home will benefit from an organization system developed for the efficient arrangement of stuff. These small organizational units will consist of items that serve a related purpose. These items should be kept together in a specific storage location such as drawers, containers or boxes. This will make it easier to find them. If you are in need of a pair of scissors, you won't have to go searching through the toolbox in the garage; instead you can look through the small organization box containing sewing tools. When you are looking for the blue flash drive containing your son's graduation photos, you won't have to launch a search party to find it under the bed. It will be there lying in the drawer under the computer table. Doesn't that sound like the kind of life you want to live?

Organizing your belongings into smaller units with similar functions helps you keep stock of what you own, what you need and what you should release. It's only when you gather all the duct tape you own into one place that you realize there are three other rolls that you completely forgot about. This technique will help you curb the accumulation of materials that can grow into a clutter if left unchecked.

Once you've gathered all these supplies into their various groups, it's time to throw away the excess. Five hammers, sevens pairs of scissors, ten cutlery sets, and all these for a family of four. Do you really need all of these items in your home? Cut down the number of your possessions until you arrive at a more reasonable number. Reclaim your space from all of this excess. Go through these collections and save only the favorites.

6. Let in one and let another go Decluttering can turn out to be a very frustrating process for people who haven't learned to control the inflow of stuff into their lives. You might have done everything perfectly, from categorizing your stuff and put them into their appropriate containers to keeping all your surfaces clear, but you may still find there is a lack of progress. There's still clutter in some parts of the house. You might wonder why that is. Think of your home as a hole and you hold a shovel, digging out sand from the hole. You dig as hard as you can and exclaim with joy once you see your hole is bigger than ever, with more space than you could have ever imagined. Now picture someone else shoveling in more sand just minutes after you've finished. Soon the hole gets filled up again. This is what seems to happen when some of us declutter. We end up almost exactly where we began. We clear away excess but then find ourselves *still* with excess. It doesn't matter how much sand you remove if you end up filling it with more sand later.

To prevent this from happening, do one simple thing: whenever you buy something new, get rid of something old. For every new book that finds its way into your personal library, your least favorite will leave the library. It is as simple as that. If a brand new ceramic bowl finds a space in the kitchen shelf, an older one should be given away.

7. Establish workable routines: At this point, due to the growing excitement that comes with picturing a decluttered home, you might think you have gotten all the principles at your fingertips. Yes, we have been able to thoroughly examine some of them, but it doesn't stop there. Decluttering isn't a one-off activity where when we are done, we are done for life. Clutter is always waiting at your doorstep getting ready to invade again. You have to be on the constant lookout. It is just like a weed. You can cut it down as much as you want but until the root is addressed, it will always rear its ugly head again. The root of clutter is in your habits. What differentiates a minimalist from a non-minimalist are good habits. To succeed at minimalism, you must change the habits that govern your everyday life.

Vigilance is key. Live intentionally. Remember to always act as a gatekeeper and protect your home from excesses. Allow these principles to become second nature to you until you can no longer exist in the presence of the slightest clutter. Block unnecessary ads on your browser if you're materialistic and easily influenced by ads. Pay off debt and allow your mind to become more free. Cancel subscriptions that are no longer necessary for your business so your mail can stay organized.

Practice your decluttering process until you become nearly perfect. You may decide on a one-day-at-a-time approach. Dispose of one item each day. It won't take much effort or time. Just be consistent with it until you master it and it becomes part of you. One day you will discover that you have the drive to dispose of more than just one item. Once your donation or trash box is full, send it off to its specified destination.

Finally, set decluttering goals in your journal so that you know how much progress you are making. Tick off your goals as you achieve them as a form of self-encouragement and motivation. Don't forget to appreciate yourself for the efforts made once you hit a new milestone. Celebrate your resilience throughout the process and your mind will be fired up to do more. Just make sure you have fun with the process. See it as a game - a game that is capable of changing your life.

Questions You Must Ask Yourself Before You Buy Anything

A lot of people in this modern world are only trying to make more money so they can buy more stuff. And some others are even trying to pay off the debt they accumulated the last time they splurged. Don't get tangled up in this way of life. It is a cycle that never ends. To ensure you prevent this from happening, ask yourself the following questions whenever you feel the urge to buy something:

1. **Am I financially equipped for this purchase**

This is where it begins. If you don't have the money for the purchase, why are you considering it in the first place? Consider the debt this might put on you. And consider what you're giving up by buying this product. If you buy this now, it means you can't buy something else down the road. Will this lead to you skipping a meal or having to live without a more essential product?

2. **Do I need this or am I just buying it because it's on sale**

Impulse purchases are one of the biggest killers of minimalism and one of the biggest magnets for clutter. A genuine need will come up again and again. If it doesn't, then you can do without the item that satisfies that urge. Make sure that all your purchases are planned and not just a spur of the moment decision. Don't just buy it as soon as you want it; give yourself time to assess your situation and budget completely. If you're buying it for a valid reason and it's a necessary purchase, you will know.

3. **Do I already own something similar to this or can it easily be rented**

Before you run off to buy something new, check to confirm that you don't already own something similar to it at home. You'll find some items in your home can be repurposed. Instead of going out to get some new containers, why not use the older ones that can just be washed and reused? If you are in need of a power tool to carry out a project, you can easily rent or borrow one from a neighbor instead of buying a whole new tool that will likely only be used once every half-year. By renting or reusing, you are saving yourself a whole lot of money.

4. If I don't buy a higher quality product, what's the likelihood I'll have to replace this?

'Quality over quantity' should be one of your mantras. The quality of the product should be your major priority because if you end up with something substandard, you'll have to shell out money for another one very soon. Why not save yourself the stress and buy something that will last a whole lot longer? Ask yourself: "Is the quality worth the price?" Maybe you want to get a new set of upholstery and you notice that the stitches are already coming undone on one side. Before spending all your money, consider using it to get something more long-lasting. It is pure joy seeing an item you bought years ago still serving its purpose with little to no wear and tear.

The 30-Day Wishlist Strategy

One way to tackle unnecessary purchases is by employing the 30 day wishlist strategy. The method here is simple: every time you feel the need to purchase something, write the name of that item on a list. This list can be anywhere: your phone, your journal, or even a note on the fridge. Each time you jot down an item, write down next to it what the date is. This will serve as a record of your spending urges and the day you felt each one. What you're going to do is wait at least 30 days before you consider buying this item. This will give you a lot of time to research the item and to see if you still want it after a lot of time has passed. For more expensive purchases, consider stretching 30 days to a longer period of time. If you decide you still want the item after 30 days or more, and you're sure you don't already own an item similar, then go ahead and buy it.

A Short message from the Author:

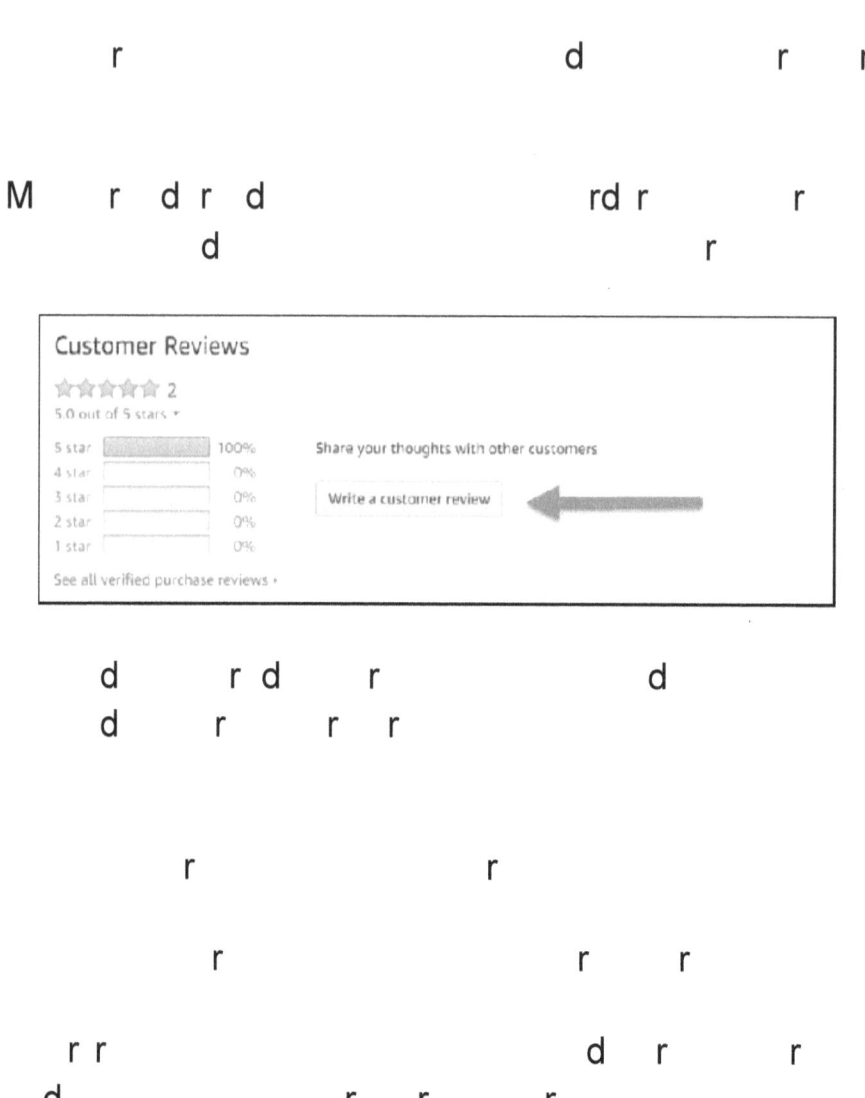

CHAPTER FOUR - FREE YOURSELF FROM EMOTIONAL AND MENTAL CLUTTER

We handled various ways in which we can take care of physical clutter, but clutter does not end there. Clutter occurs in our mind too. When people complain about emotional instability or depression, it is simply because of emotional clutter. They have ignored the main focus of existence and have begun chasing the meaningless things in life - things that only clog the mind and lead nowhere.

The building blocks of the mind are thoughts. Once our thoughts have been managed, then mind clutter can be dealt with. These thoughts can be positive, negative or neutral and just like your home is cluttered with possessions, your mind can also become cluttered with thoughts. If they are positive thoughts, then you are on the safe side. But that is not usually the case. Unfortunately it is not as easy to deal with mental and emotional clutter as it is to deal with physical clutter. You can't just discard a thought and expect it to not return. It doesn't work that way.

Sometimes it seems like these thoughts have mechanisms and minds of their own, and they can sometimes control you. Constructive thinking is necessary to help out with problem-solving, analyses, decision making, and planning, but despite all of this, the mind can produce negativity out of nowhere. This forms an inner distraction from the physical world around you. Have you ever come across someone on the subway that went past their designated stop just because they were deep in their thoughts? That signifies a dangerous emotional clutter. They are gradually losing touch with the physical world. These negative thoughts mostly spring up as a result of assuming that the harder you think about your predicaments, the easier it will be for you to get out them. Of course, we know perfectly well that it is a flawed ideology, yet we hold on to it. Why? It is because these thoughts have already created a stronghold in the mind.

Soon you discover that you have been caught up in a constant loop of regretful thinking about your past and anxiety for the future.

These thoughts become such an integral part of your mind that you begin to think that there is nothing that can be done about it. You can't just shut down your brain and have it stop processing some thoughts. Negative thoughts are like a virus on a computer. You can reboot the system and it's still there when you turn it back on. You can sleep, wake up again, and your thoughts will continue to bother you. You have to deal with them squarely before you ruin your week.

All of your thoughts might be unconscious, but you can manage them by practicing intentionality. You have far more control over your mind than you think. You just have to be willing to exercise that control. Once you've managed your emotional clutter, you will discover an immense amount of creativity and inspiration that awaits you, hidden under all of that clutter.

Factors that Facilitate Mental Clutter

Before we set about trying to deal with mental and emotional clutter, it is necessary that we tackle the root problem. Where does all of this clutter emanate from?

- **Stress**

Stress can easily overwhelm you and overpower your motivation to live. Stress is associated with a variety of mental issues such as depression, anxiety and panic attacks. When combined with worries, negative thoughts and other concerns that burden our daily life, the problem only multiplies. Sleep becomes affected. Anger management issues may set in. Headaches and chest pains become the order of the day.

The stress can manifest itself in a variety of ways, for example, in a toxic work environment, domestic violence at home, or even a problematic child. Things turn out to be so complicated and intense that your mind loses the ability to control itself.

- **An Excess of Material Objects**

We handled this in a preceding chapter. Once your life and home become too clogged and cluttered with stuff, your mind begins to suffer. In the modern age, we are so eager to fill up our homes with useless possessions that have no true value and can be done without. All of this stuff contributes to time consumption, becomes a financial drain and induces anxiety.

People who are propelled to live their lives based on the quantity of physical possessions they own are always on the competitive side. Nothing is ever enough for them. They will always want to keep up with the latest trends no matter what it will cost them financially or emotionally. Decluttering your life of these things will ultimately help to curb the effects of negative thinking and anxiety.

- **A Litany of Choices**

Too much choice and variety can subtly lead to depression and anxiety. At first it might seem like the perfect life, to have a load of choices to decide from, but upon a closer analysis you will discover the unadmirable quality of it. What should be a decision that can be made in mere seconds will lead to days of agonizing contemplation. A litany of choices is brain-draining and stressful.

Must-Know Practices to Help You Deal with Mental Clutter

1. **Meditation**

Certain misconceptions may deter you from practicing meditation. Truth is, you don't have to be a Buddhist monk, a psychic, or even a certified witch to practice meditation. Don't get scared by the stories you hear about cave dwellers who meditate for months at a time. There are levels of meditation, and at this point, we are only going to tackle the basic levels of it. Meditation does not belong to people of a certain religious faith or spiritual inclination.

The only thing is that meditation and the reason for performing it vary from one meditator to another. For this chapter, meditation will be considered a tool to help you control your mind and your thoughts. You can practice meditation anywhere you feel like it. You don't necessarily need a quiet environment, but you must be able to achieve that quietness on the inside. That way, it will be easier for you to sort through your thoughts and pick out those that should be discarded. The benefits of practicing meditation are numerous, both for your physical wellbeing and also for the emotional side of your life.

The main point is to practice meditation consistently. You cannot reap its full benefits without constant practice. Commit to practicing meditation at a scheduled time every single day. That way, you will improve your ability to control your mind mechanisms and put them in check.

Meditation doesn't have to take long. All you have to do is to find a spot and sit still. Set out a specific time every day that you will carry out your meditation and stick to it. Don't choose an overly comfortable position so that you don't fall asleep while meditating. Turn off every digital device that's capable of producing noise or any distractions. Try and time yourself, so you know when you have done enough. For beginners, five minutes is enough time to meditate effectively.

Make sure you are ready for the process, and nothing else will distract you. For the next five minutes, focus on your breathing. Count the number of breaths you take in and out of your body. Notice how the air leaves you and returns into your nostrils. Observe the rise and fall of your chest region. Allow your breath to flow naturally; don't try to control them. This will help you build focus. At first, you might encounter problems keeping focus but try and return your attention to your breathing each time.

Close your eyes to avoid visual distractions. The goal of meditation is to shut thoughts out of your mind. By focusing on the breath, you are taking attention away from anything that causes you stress. Wave off the negative and store the positives so you can ruminate on them when the time finally arrives.

2. **Deal with the negative thoughts**

A lot of people go through life everyday with negative thoughts floating across the surface of their minds. They have become victims of a mental flood and if care is not taken, they may drown. The negative voices in their heads speak louder and louder until they can't even hear themselves. This form of negativity can be given strength and a stronghold in the mind if it is not challenged at the initial stage.

The first step is to notice these thoughts before they get out of control. Notice the pattern with which they operate in your mind. You can employ these strategies to help you out:

a. **Be Watchful**

You don't always need to have an emotional reaction to all your thoughts. Sometimes you should take yourself out of the scene and become a spectator. Observe what is going on in your mind. Notice how your thoughts interact with one another. Don't judge any of these thoughts negatively or positively. Just sit back and observe.

b. **See your thoughts for what they really are**

Although they are powerful enough to alter whole facets of your life, understand these are thoughts and nothing more. They are not real for the time being, but they have the capability to become real if you don't manage them.

c. **Put up a roadblock**

You own your mind, right? They you should be able to determine what comes in, what stays and what goes out. Whenever you catch yourself in a mental state that makes you uncomfortable, learn to scold yourself and stop the reaction. You can be vocal about your refusal to think those thoughts. Say, "I refuse to be caught by negative thoughts in this web of distractions." Build walls around your mind, strongholds that will serve to protect you whenever the time arrives.

d. **Know the causes**

Every negative thought in your mind is caused or triggered by a certain factor. It could be a person, another thought, a situation or even a physical state. The next time you find yourself wallowing in these thoughts, take the time to find out what triggered the thoughts. Chances are that they will be lying there waiting to be discovered and dealt with.

Write down the major triggers that come to your mind. Brood over them for a while and see if you can find any solutions to them. If it's something that you can solve by yourself, such as the reconciliation of a wrecked relationship or working on your own flaws, then go ahead and deal with these thoughts. If you discover that you have no power over the situation at hand such as an inability to travel because of bad weather or a miscarriage, make up your mind to be happy regardless. You caused none of it so there is no need to feel bad about it.

f. **Occupy your mind**

Each day you wake, you wake up with a clear mind, a tabula rasa. If you leave it empty, the mind has a way of creating something to do for its own self. Ever noticed how your mind is never empty, how at every point in time you are always ruminating and considering an issue? The mind is only inactive when you are asleep, and that is if it doesn't get overwhelmed by dreams. So once you wake up, give your mind something creative to do. Focus your brainpower on important projects that will help fulfill a long term goal. Give yourself something positive to worry about, like how you can get a PhD. If you find yourself stuck in traffic, pick up a book, and read or search for an insightful TED talk and listen to it.

3. **Subdue your mind under your control**

You are the boss here. Your mind belongs to you, and you should never give up control. Never let it run through the thoughts you don't want to process. Get your mind under control so that each time, you are pleased by the outcome it produces. You can achieve this by practicing the following:

a. **Identifying the wrong thoughts and replacing them**: The wrong thoughts are easy to identify; they can be spotted from miles away. Once your mind begins to process them, you notice a certain kind of weight hovering over you. And they are mostly exaggerated. Funny enough, the wrong thoughts are very pleasing to hold. You just lost your job at 50, and you begin to think, "I am a total failure. Can anything good come out of me?" You know you should not be thinking that way, but it seems very comfortable to dwell in that state of mind. Why? Well, no one thinks positive thoughts after a bad experience. If you examine that thought closely and truthfully, you will discover that it is not entirely true. Somebody somewhere admires you for who you are irrespective of your current financial state.

Instead of keeping yourself in that state, why not challenge your negative thoughts with positive ones? Reassure yourself that you are not a failure or a loser. Thinking you are one will not automatically make you a success. How many times have you gone into a job interview and one of the interviewers says, "Well, it seems you have always thought of yourself as a failure. We are going to give you the job to help you stop seeing yourself that way." It doesn't happen. In fact, people who breed negative thoughts are always repulsive to others. For every person who has given a negative comment about you or your work, there are about ten more making positive remarks. So why are you allowing that one comment to spoil your mood and corrupt your other thoughts?

b. **Accept the situation but don't get comfortable with it**

What do you do when the negative thoughts swirling around your mind are true? How will you be able to cope with the situation triggering these negative thoughts? It is hard to challenge negative thoughts with positivity when the truth is staring right at you. You just lost your home and all of your property to fire. Your grades are going down the drain and at this rate you are probably not going to graduate.

These are negative thoughts about situations that cannot be eliminated, but you can reduce the effect that they have on your mind by accepting the situation at hand, not the thoughts. It happened, and there is nothing you can do about the past, but you can change the future. Don't begin to nurture guilt about your carelessness, or go on about how things could have been better. You are only making your head foggier and clogging up your emotions. At this point, your best bet for a solution is to find peace of mind.

Accepting the situation will help you identify ways to improve or solve the problem at hand. There is always a brighter side, no matter how dim it may be, and it can only be identified with a clear mind.

c. **Take necessary actions**
Worrying and strategizing are two different things. Worrying is easier but its results can be bad for you. Strategy requires mental energy that most of us are not willing to sacrifice. The truth is that

worry gets you nowhere; it is better you employ strategy. The downside of worry is that you expend so much energy producing negative thoughts and you never come up with a solution. All that energy you spent worrying could have been put towards strategizing, and perhaps your problem would be fixed by now.

Identify Your Core Values

A major challenge that people of this age face is the inability to identify what is truly important to their existence. In our world today, there are so many distractions that take away from what we need. We are bombarded by marketing and meaningless messages, and we rarely go inward, connecting to our inner voice. These things can become such an overload that the process of prioritizing our values becomes a major task. This makes it very necessary to reevaluate what is most important to us with each passing day. Rise over all of the societal noise by defining your core values.

Identifying your core values is one sure way to help you combat clutter, both physically and mentally. These principles will help you spend time, energy, and money doing the things that help you in the long run. The presence of core values enables you to keep focus. It is easier to spot distractions. A lot of the highest achievers of our age are people who have identified their core values. Once, during an interview, Steve Jobs stated that he kept his wardrobe streamlined to simple black turtlenecks, blue jeans, and New Balance sneakers. Why? So that his wardrobe decisions didn't take up a lot of brainpower and he could focus on what really matters. That reply reflects the mindset of someone who has identified his core values. Try to picture how organized and minimalistic his closet probably looked.

How to Identify Your Core Values

Core values are not selected; they are discovered or revealed. It is easy to say that physical fitness is one of your core values, but when was the last time you actually exercised?

Deciding on your core values can be a daunting task, but what you find out about yourself will help you. In case you are unfamiliar with the core values terrain, let's go through some lists and identify some values that appeal to you. From there, you can streamline them into your perfect options. These can help you identify your core values:

a. Your peak experiences

What do you consider a very important moment in your life? What makes that moment standout for you? What happened to you in that very moment? What values came into play to make this moment a very important one?

b. Suppressed values

This is the opposite of the first one. Here, consider the values that cruised through you when you were the most angry and irritated. What got you angry during those moments? Those are your suppressed values. They never seem to rear their heads but they are there as relevant as ever.

c. Brainstorming

Brainstorming involves more of a general search. You ask yourself questions that only you can answer. Pick a pen and a jotter and provide answers to these questions:

- What values in others attracts me the most?
- What drives me the most in life?
- What do I admire most about myself?
- What's one virtue I never want to lose?

While answering these questions, you will certainly run into moments of clarity and understanding and you will find your core values waiting on the other side of reflection.

d. Ask the people around you

Sometimes people around you notice things you might ignore about yourself. For example, someone who is neat or organized might not necessarily understand how neat or organized he or she is until people point it out and commend them for it. It is just like using a particular cologne brand for years. Soon the fragrance blends in naturally with your nose and your olfactory nerves fail to interpret the smell because they have been doing so for a long time. Until the day someone points it out to you, you might never understand how much it has become a part of you.

Your core values are like this. People see your values before you even notice them, so their opinions can be very necessary for helping you identify these values. Look for the smart and observant people around you and ask them to define you and what they think you stand for. You will be amazed by the responses you receive. There is no way that you won't be able to identify your core values after following these steps.

Everything You Need to Know About Decluttering Your Relationships

You need people in your life, but they can sometimes be great hindrances. Once your relationships begin to falter, an unbalance sets in and soon, you're overcome by distress. The painful question, "Who can I trust?" begins to haunt you.

A popular saying goes, "We disagree to agree." Misunderstandings and reconciliations are some of the blocks that build and strengthen a relationship. But when these interactions constantly leave you worn out and emotionally drained, then it's high time you either try to mend broken bridges or remove the other party from your life.

You will never understand the importance of having healthy relationships until you try to imagine a life without any form of anxiety relating to the people in it. The most productive people are those who have created a perfect balance in every relationship, be it their relationship with their spouse, children, bosses or even the person beside them on the train.

Relationship clutter can build up in a variety of ways such as minor-major arguments, malice keeping, hatred, envy, jealousy, and the likes. Once they gain enough ground, they clog up your mind. Think back to the last time you felt annoyed by your best friend, or when you envied someone so much that you could taste the gall in your own throat. Think back and consider how heavy your heart felt in those moments. Then try to remember the feeling you had when there was an embrace of reconciliation. Can you feel how light your heart was in that moment and the deep breaths you took afterward? That's the beauty of a decluttered mind. Space is instantly created for something else, something worthwhile.

It is not just about having relationships but having quality relationships. Here's another saying: "It is better to make one true friend in a thousand years than to make one thousand fake acquaintances in one year." The beauty of relationships is not in quantity but in quality. The ingredients that make up a great friendship will include:

- Shared Interests
- Mutual respect and trust
- Understanding and acceptance
- Openness and honesty
- Healthy conflict resolution

Creating relationships is necessary to your existence and this is why it is essential to take your time choosing the relationships you should invest in. The primary reason why the loss of a relationship hurts so much is because of our emotional investment.

To begin with, work on your relationships. Start with yourself. They say, "If you want to change the world, start with yourself." If you want to change your relationships, you should start with yourself. It might be so obvious and glaring that the other person in the relationship needs to make a change too, but ignore that fact and start with your own change. It will help you heal and do away with all the clutter. After all, you can't change others except if they agree to change themselves or be changed. These strategies will help you build healthier relationships:

1. INVEST YOURSELF YOUR TIME AND PRESENCE

Once I saw someone post a picture of a friend and caption it, "Thank you for being there. Happy Birthday." It was the first time I had seen such a short message used on a birthday post, but it was very profound. That word 'there' meant so much to the person who had posted the picture. But what exactly did he or she mean by 'there'?

'There' signifies presence and time. That friend was available when he was most needed. Those kinds of friends are hard to ignore or forget. They make themselves available during the darkest times of our lives. They are present when it matters. How present are you in your relationships? How much of yourself have you invested? Here is how to invest yourself into a relationship:
   1. Pay Attention

How do you feel when someone isn't paying any attention to something important you are saying? How does it feel when you know they aren't listening to something that means a lot to you? It is disheartening at best, and the chances that you will ever want to share a conversation with them are very slim. The truth, as bitter as it may sound, is that you have probably done it too, intentionally or unintentionally.

This mostly happens because of the numerous distractions in the mind that tend to monopolize your attention. This causes you to focus more on the crowd in your mind than on the person talking to you. Still, that is no excuse. Paying attention is the willingness to step out of all those distractions and listen, not just hear. Absorb the speaker and their words so that he or she will feel safe and comfortable talking to you. Make it all about the other person and what they are saying. Make each gesture count and try not to look distracted. These tips will help:

- Allow the speaker to dominate the conversation until they ask for your opinion
- Avoid unnecessary interruptions, except if you have something really important to say.
- Hear the full story before jumping to conclusions.
- Keep your gestures and facial expressions as neutral as possible.

Paying attention might look one-sided, like the speaker is the only one who benefits during the interaction, but learning to listen and shut out the noise in your mind is a huge benefit to you. In fact, it is one way of helping you declutter your mind and be more present.

a. Positive speaking and encouragement

Language matters in every conversation. Don't rush to spill the contents of your mind. First, probe them and anticipate a reaction before you release them. Negative comments are products of negative thoughts and can be damaging to a relationship.

Pay close attention to the things you say during a conversation. It might not seem to matter, but the other person may feel differently.

Recognize that each word is powerful and can create a different effect to what was intended. Don't say, "But you should have known better, especially with all of your education." Say, "It was a learning moment for you, and I am happy you learned the lesson." Don't say, "You acted so stupidly." Say, "I don't think that was the right thing to do at that moment." Speak with love and compassion.

Mastering the art of compassionate communication will make others want to talk and relate to you. Resist the temptation to be judgmental about other people's actions. Put yourself in their shoes and try to understand why they act the way they do. When you master the art of being kind in all forms, the people around you will mirror the same actions, and your relationships will blossom further. Of course, you already have an idea of how good that will be for your emotions. You will find peace in your inner world, and it will reflect into the world around you.

    b. Find reasons to love

No matter how bad a person is, there is always one reason to love them. Find that reason and cling to it. Of course, we have been told to love people unconditionally, but human nature makes that hard to do. Sometimes it is best to find reasons to love them even when it seems like they should not be loved. Reducing the negative thoughts you have about people in your life can significantly improve your relationship with them.

Studies have shown that when we think positively about others, it leads to increased contentment in life, kindness towards others in general, hope and enthusiasm to build better relationships. How you decide to practice the art of positive thinking is up to you. You can do it by meditating on their good characters, or you can do it by saying positive things about them. The point of this practice is to transform your mind and declutter your emotions.

c. Eliminate comparison

Comparison is a prison that many people are locked in. Comparing yourself to others is one sure way to hold you back from any form of progress. Comparisons are fertile ground for breeding negative thoughts. "Am I good enough?" "Do I have what it takes to be admired like he or she is?" "Will I ever be that attractive?"

These thoughts can build up and get out of control until low self-esteem takes control of your thoughts. Most times, constant comparison can also lead to mild hatred for the person you are comparing yourself to. There is a high possibility of you viewing them as the reason for your unhappiness, even when this is an entirely unfair accusation. And there is no way you can have a healthy relationship with someone whom you feel this way about. Each time you see them, something shifts inside of you. Your mind begins to act abnormally.

You are on your own journey in life, and only you can understand your struggles. This is why we handled the issue of core values. A person who has discovered his or her true core values cannot be affected by comparisons to others because they already have a focus. Other people's journeys don't affect them.

Don't get me wrong, from time to time comparisons can take a positive turn, and that is something you should be on the lookout for. Use comparisons to motivate yourself and work harder to become a better person. Comparisons can help you identify places in your life that need to be worked on and improved. But when you begin to notice its excesses, and it takes a negative turn, turn it down a little. The mental effort involved in comparisons can drain you. Never allow it to grow out of your control. These tips can help you combat comparison:

- [ ] Accept Yourself

You are perfect the way you are, not because you are actually perfect but because you choose to believe that you are perfect. You can't change anything about yourself unless you have hundreds of dollars stashed up somewhere to spend on plastic surgery. Good luck with that and I only pray that you don't come out looking more messed up than before.

Instead of battling to change who you are, you can do a quick job of accepting yourself. No amount of comparison or worry will change who you are. Most people are more receptive to people who have accepted themselves for who they are. Self-acceptance is self-liberation and self-empowerment.

- [ ] Improve what needs to be improved

Change the things about yourself that can be changed. Are you insecure about your appearance? Work on your wardrobe or your hairstyle. Have you noticed that more people are attracted to someone who smiles? Then try to have more gentle facial expressions. Sometimes, no matter how much you try, you might never be able to match up to the people you admire and compare yourself to. Don't sweat it. Simply find something that makes you exceptional and work on it. Your core values and life priorities should be the main factor in helping you define your life. Sometimes we are attracted to qualities in others that we don't need. She has longer legs. So what, are you trying to become a long jumper? You are a writer, so the longer legs shouldn't matter to you. Focus on your strengths, the things that make you unique. Somebody out there that you don't even know yet thinks you are awesome because of them.

- [ ] Practice Gratitude

I talked about this in chapter three, but it still remains an important tip. You can forget to feel gratitude when you become too focused on what another person has. You begin to ignore the beautiful things that life has brought your way, simply because you are missing out on some other little things.

Gratitude is about committing to the bright side. It's a commitment to creating joy even when it feels like there's none at all. There are good things in your life and they should never be ignored. Focus on them for at least three to five minutes every day before going to bed or after waking up. I advise making gratitude part of your morning routine since it's a great way to start your day, but if you have busy mornings, a nightly gratitude routine works just fine as well. Take a moment to think about how blessed you are. It can be surprisingly liberating.

2. RELEASE YOURSELF FROM YOUR PAST

Carrying the burdens of the past is one way to hold yourself back from seeing the light in your relationships and life, in general. You may have been in some toxic relationships before now, but there is a time to let these lingering feelings go. It is natural for the mind to keep replaying scenarios and hurt over and over. However, this process should not take over any part of our lives. Having these memories return over and over can create wells of anger, guilt, and shame. These thoughts keep you stuck to the past, drain the positivity in the present, and rob your future. You not only clutter your emotions; you also imprison your mind and hinder its productivity.

It is hard to let go of pain from the past, but it can still be done. A lot of people have succeeded in doing it. You can, too. The benefits of letting go are enormous. Not only will you have more positivity because you create positivity, but you will likely also see more positive things come into your life. Why? Because we are a magnet for our life circumstances. Exude positivity, and you'll attract positivity. So, step one, let go of your past. Try the following tips:

a. Make Resolutions and Stick to Them

People get a strange amount of comfort from wallowing in pain, but we should always resist this urge. It gets nothing solved. Sometimes the people you feel have hurt you have no idea that they ever did that. Take action and find ways to resolve any issue that you feel needs to be resolved. Take out time to communicate with the person and clear the air. No matter how fresh the hurt is, you should try to talk things out instead of bearing a useless burden and clogging your mind.

Don't go into the reconciliation process with a bitter heart. That will only make the dialogue process difficult. Healthy communication is paramount for you to reach a sensible solution; if not, your discussion may be hostile. Most of the process will involve listening to the other party's grievances and understanding how you hurt them. There will be apologies and a call to forgiveness, then a final resolution.

Keep an open mind while discussing and resolving issues. When you dwell on your hurt, your perspective begins to feel like the only true angle, but this is not true at all. Be flexible and see things from another person's perspective. Put yourself in other people's shoes. Ask yourself questions, such as:

- What exactly made this person get angry and say what he or she said?
- What actions or words of yours were misinterpreted and taken the wrong way?
- Is there a possibility you've interpreted the situation in the wrong way?

Be flexible enough to challenge your own point of view. Rigidity does not help you in your empathy, it only clings to its own beliefs, even when they are incorrect and unhelpful. Compromise your stance for the sake of your friendships.

b. Forgiveness

They might never ask for forgiveness, but forgive anyway. This is for your sake as well, not just the other person's. The more people you vow not to forgive, the more files and tabs are open in the browser of your mind. Imagine how slow your computer would be, if it was invested in so many needless things as your mind. It is time to close some tabs! Clinging to all that trash only makes you suffer. Free yourself now!

Forgiveness doesn't mean you're playing the fool and allowing someone to come into your life and hurt you again. Forgiveness is letting go of all resentment and anger so you are no longer holding onto poison. Forgiveness is hard to give when the other party still hasn't taken responsibility for their actions. Understand that they are on a lower level of understanding and there is no need to stoop so low or act on their level.

CHAPTER FI E THE SECRETS OF FINANCIAL MINIMALISM

As new as it may sound to you, financial minimalism is a real concept, and it comes with real benefits. Some of us might have even practiced it without knowing that we were being financially minimalistic. While most of us focus on decluttering our homes and our physical environment, minimalism can also be applied to financial health. All the times you restrained yourself from spending extravagantly, that was financial minimalism. Enrolling in a cashless economy is financial minimalism.

Budgeting, which is a major aspect of financial minimalism, will give more clarity on your spending and help you with your financial priorities. Financial minimalism is not about spending less money, but about only spending money when you need to. It advocates against spending whenever you feel like it. Financial minimalism is about spending intentionally, keeping control of every penny, and not letting any amount slip through your fingers.

How Minimalism Can Help You Financially

1. Financial minimalism helps you to minimize your spending

With financial minimalism, you're only going to purchase the items or services that mean the most to you. Once you have set your purchasing priorities straight, you will naturally have more control over your spending habits. The way you spend money changes when you are focused on acquiring specific items and not just living on a spur-of-the-moment basis. When you spend more intentionally, you naturally begin to save more money.

2. Less excess in your home

Once you are able to control your spending, you automatically control the accumulation of excess in your life. Financial minimalism helps you keep track of the things you already own so you don't continue to buy the same thing, creating clutter. You'll see the results of your intentional spending in the space you live in. Over time, less clutter will form and you'll manage your space far more easily.

3. Gives you more focus for your financial goals

Financial minimalism helps you understand the importance of a financial budget. You spend with a plan, with an aim. Budgeting helps to streamline your spending based on your current needs. It will also help you to identify areas where you have to change the way you handle money. With less money coming out of your accounts, it's much easier to keep your financial goals in sight.

4. Freedom from debt

A good way to simplify your financial life is to get out of debt. In fact, it's difficult to get control over your finances if you still have a lot of debt. Debt can have the same effect on your finances as negative thinking does on your mind. With financial minimalism, it will be easy for you to pinpoint the factors that lead to debt accumulation and tackle them. And on top of this, you will be in a much better position to pay off debt now that you're saving more money due to your new minimalist lifestyle.

5. Giving becomes easier for you

When you have more financial security, you're able to give more without restriction. You're spending less on yourself, so you can give to others when they need it. When you practice financial minimalism, it is easier for you to recognize what and how much of it you can give. While budgeting for the month, you can cut down on some expenses and donate the extra money instead. That way you keep track of your money and know that nothing was wasted.

Minimalist Tips to Help You Achieve Financial Freedom

1. **Identify your financial values**

You must know the things that are important to you when it comes to money. It will be difficult for you to gain control over your finances if you haven't understood your values yet. Have a clear picture of the money habits in your life that needs to be eliminated. Pick out those that need to be adopted and work on assimilating them into your habits. Discover what your financial values are and start streamlining your budget to suit them. Some practices that you can adopt are:

- Never living above your means
- Eliminating the propensity to borrow
- Sticking to a budget
- Having an emergency fund

With these new practices in your life, it will be easier for you to cut out the non-essentials among your spending. Your financial goals will be reached with less stress and life becomes even simpler.

2. **Have an emergency fund**

Having an emergency fund is always a lifesaver. The amount you deposit into it will depend on how much you earn, and no matter how small your income is, make sure that a percentage of it goes into the emergency fund. Transfer money into your emergency fund and then carry on with the rest of the month. Don't think of it as another source of money for whenever you want to spend. As its name suggests, it is reserved for emergencies. You have to practice thorough discipline if you want to be successful with it. Whenever you have to take from it, make sure you add more money into it later to maintain a reasonable balance.

3. **Employ digital help**

There are many fantastic apps in the app store that will help you pay your bills automatically without causing you any stress. All you need is to input your payment method, the scheduled time for the payment, and the amount to be paid. A few days before the payment is to be made, you will be alerted about the incoming deductions. Some of these apps will also help you keep track of how much you spent on a particular service over a period of time. By making full use of these apps, you never have to worry about making a payment on time (and potentially creating debt!), and you save a little bit of time every month.

4. **Develop a budgeting system that works and stick to it**

Do you want to spend less than you make? Then the solution is simple: you need a budget. Budgeting helps you to manage expenses and never spend more than you can afford. Regardless of how much you make, the money that leaves your hands every month should never be more than what comes in; if it is, you stand a risk of running into more debt. It sounds like something everyone should be able to do easily, but this isn't the case at all.

Group your expenses into categories to help you keep track of how much you spend on each category. Keep the categories as consolidated as possible, so the list doesn't grow too long. Common categories include utilities, phone bills, transportation, rent, food, and miscellaneous. The contents of the list will differ from person to person due to various reasons, but they should share streamlined equality. Brainstorm and estimate how much you spend for each category per month and use that to create your final budget.

It is one thing to have a budget; it is another thing to stick to it. Don't create a budget for the sake of creating a budget. Resist the urge to sit back and suddenly feel that everything is going to be okay. Your work is not done! Discipline should bind you to your budget. Temptations will arise and try to surface your old habits, so prepare yourself for this. Keep your focus on your core financial values, and you will always come out successful.

5. **Minimize debt**

Simply put, "Debt is money stolen from your future savings." And who said time travel wasn't a thing, when people are stealing from their future selves every day. You can always find the discipline to prevent yourself from falling into debt, no matter how tight the situation may seem. Seek out other options. Shift your mentality towards owning things that you can afford at the present moment, instead of buying things on credit and insisting you'll get your act together later. The peace of mind that comes from having no debt is far more rewarding than the fleeting high your spur-of-the-moment purchase gave you.

6. **Find the best deals**

Whenever you need to purchase something, take your time to research and find the best deals around. It may take a little bit of time, but the end result is worth it. You'll still get the exact same thing, but you'll be spending less money. Don't be so hasty to spend your hard-earned dollars just because you can afford it. Saving some money by finding the best deal will leave you with more money after the transaction. You can put this towards your savings or purchase something else that you need. You'll be amazed by the number of discounts offered. You just have to find them. And remember, although you should go for the best deal, make sure it is still for a high or above-average quality product.

7. **Get rid of distractions**

Think deeply and try to identify all the potential distractions from your financially minimalist life. What are the temptations that push you to buy things that you do not need? If you're subscribed to a particular store that always sends you compelling articles that lead you to buy their products, then unsubscribe. Unfollow social media influencers that are constantly tempting you into buying new products you don't need. If there is something or someone in your life, making you feel like your life is incomplete, remove that trigger. You won't be sorry and you won't be lesser for it. With these distractions out of the way, you can finally focus all your attention on doing right by your finances and your life.

CHAPTER SI - ADVANCED HOME DECLUTTERING

Now it's time for you to put all your new decluttering skills to work. In this chapter, we will be going through the various rooms in the house. I will be providing you with some tips on how to get rid of the excess in these rooms and defeat clutter instantly. Start from the room that feels most comfortable to you or the room with the most clutter. It is your call. Just make sure you actually begin the process and keep up with it. You don't have to follow the exact order I am going to detail here. At this point, the decluttering principles we studied in chapter three will be very important. Use them to guide you through the decluttering process of each room. The tips in this chapter will only be the basics.

A Room-by-Room Decluttering Guide
1. LIVING ROOM

First, visualize your living room as you want it. Identify the furniture you want to keep and the ones that you will leave. Figure out all the things that should be on the shelves and the surface spaces.

...t, begin to ditch all of those things that will hinder your living ...om being the perfect living room. Purging unnecessary items ... a time will make a dramatic impact and transform your ...ithin days. Consider the values that each item brings ...ing-room ambiance. Ask yourself questions about ...corative objects really provide the joy and ... attributed to their presence? Have they ...? Are they a little worn? And most ... or are they gifts you just feel you

Send everything into its space. Figure out the areas to store your DVDs, games, and computer. Make sure that every other object in the sitting-room is kept in their appropriate area. All surfaces should remain clear, and stray objects should not be found on surfaces that do not belong to them. The surfaces in question include coffee tables, side tables, and desks. The sitting room floor should be kept tidy too.

Set a limit for the number of furniture and decorative materials that will exist in the sitting-room at any given time. Limit the things collected into the sitting-room. Display fewer items so that attention doesn't get divided and clutter doesn't begin to form again. This is the space in which you will be receiving guests, so stay aware of the impression your sitting-room is leaving on people who visit you.

2. BEDROOM

The bedroom is one of the most cluttered parts of the house. Since it's one of the more private rooms in the house, we think that we can do anything here and it won't matter. It does matter. Maybe not to your guests, but it is affecting your ability to rest in this room.

Before you begin to declutter, take a moment to picture what you want your bedroom to look like after the decluttering process. What kind of room do you envision? Begin to remove all the things creating clutter.

You should select items to keep, donate or trash. You will con across items that should be taken out of the room to another ro where they will serve more important purposes. Sort them into own pile and take them out later, to be arranged in their new ho

Dividing the bedroom into zones is quite easy. There will b for sleeping, dressing, and, for some, working. Sort the thi room into their various spaces and organize them neatl things you will need most often very close to you, somewhere on your bedside table.

Deal with surfaces and plan out the items that should be found on them every day. The bed is the most important surface in the room, and it is necessary for your wellbeing. It should always be kept as clear, clean, and organized as possible. Eliminate all clutter that is forming on your bed. You should also organize your wardrobe so it will be easier to handle your clothes and prevent them from finding their way onto the bed.

3. KITCHEN

The kitchen is the powerhouse of the home. If it is in disarray, everybody in the home feels it. There will be missing cutlery, broken ceramics, wafts of dust underneath the cabinets and pests in every corner. Since perishables and food are kept in this room, you must keep this space clean. Otherwise, you may start to attract unwelcome little guests, in the form of rodents or cockroaches. Due to its significance, the kitchen is filled with a lot of appliances and other tools. Once the objects in this room build into a clutter, the functionality of this space becomes undermined.

The beauty of every kitchen is in its spaciousness and the availability of clear countertops. That is what makes it desirable to cook here. Think about how lovely it will be to have your cabinets and shelves organized in the most welcoming way.

The first thing to do is empty every single cabinet or shelf in the kitchen. Even if you are sure that you will be returning an item back to this space, remove it still. You might not know how much space it is taking up just by being in that spot. Plus, removing everything provides the opportunity to clean the cabinet.

Sort through the items and find those that should be kept, donated, or trashed. When was the last time you used a particular appliance? Is it even working still? With each item you pick, ask yourself these important questions that will help you reach a conclusion about the future of each item.

If you have never categorized the items in your kitchen, you should do that now. Break them into groups such as baking items, cutting tools, everyday appliances, and mugs. Find all excess and drop them into the donation box.

Tips for Getting Rid of Sentimental Clutter

Some sentimental objects are worth keeping. Like a deceased relative's fur coat or a prized antique, but let's face it, there are some sentimental things that need to go. Do you really need your ex-boyfriend's old guitar picks? Or your mother's (no matter how deceased she may be) incredibly ugly old mugs? Probably not. Even if you know you don't want them or need them, they can still be hard to get rid of. Keep these tips in mind:

- **Eliminate all guilt**

Sometimes we don't throw away sentimental objects because we feel guilty. Think about where this guilt stems from. Is the object in question something that once belonged to an old relative? Do you feel bad because it's like you're throwing away a piece of them? Nip this thinking in the bud. People are not their possessions. Chances are you have something else from them that is far more useful and that doesn't create as much clutter. You are not harming anyone here, so don't feel guilty.

- **Focus on a different aspect of the memory**

Another reason why we keep sentimental things is because they are attached to a certain memory. This makes total sense. Luckily for you, you don't have to throw away the memory if you throw away the object. If you're throwing away an item connected to a memory, consider writing a journal entry about the memory instead. Immortalize it that way. Or look at old pictures of this memory. Let's say you're holding onto your mother's ugly mugs because she used to drink her favorite coffee out of them. Well, hold on a sec, you also live in the house where your mother used to drink her favorite coffee out of her ugly mugs. See the kitchen as the connection to this memory instead.

- **Give it to someone else**

If you know someone else who might want this item, consider giving it to them. This way, you don't have to see the object in the garbage. Someone out there still has it and still appreciates it. And if the object is something that belongs to someone else in the first place (like an ex-boyfriend), then give it back already! There's no use holding on.

The Best Way to Decorate and Design a Minimalist Home

When decorating your minimalist home, you should keep three important factors in mind:

a. Quality
b. Spaciousness
c. Clear surfaces

These factors are more important than the subjective beauty of your decorative items. By keeping these factors in mind, almost any decorative item can look appealing. Use these tips to get started:

1. Go for neutral colours

Riots of color can sometimes appear as clutter. Try to keep your color combinations as simple and neutral as possible. Go for colors that inspire a feeling of calmness, whatever that means to you. It may not be the same color for everyone, but it's rarely bright or neon color. It doesn't mean that you cannot experiment with colors and get creative; it just means you should first study the colors you want, think about how those colors affect you and find out if they work well together. Ask yourself if the combination is easy on the eyes. Remember, this is your private, resting space. It's absolutely vital that you can relax here.

2.   **uality over quantity**
You should consider each piece carefully before you let it into your home. Work with few objects while decorating your home, but make sure that every single object is of a reasonable or high quality. Your goal is to create a comfortable space that anyone would be comfortable in. Choose well-made designs that are built to last. Since you will be using these objects a lot, it is important that they will survive more than a few uses.

3.   **Bring in nature**
Florals and greenery will add a beautiful touch of nature to your sitting-room and kitchen. The colors from flowers or other plants will also add to the overall color scheme of your home. Keep this in mind when you are choosing your natural pieces. What's wonderful about plants is they bring in so much beauty and they last as long as you are able to take care of them. Hopefully, that is a long time! Be good to your plants.

4.   **Interesting accessories**
The accessories in a room can change the entire look of the room. An accessory in this regard is anything that is added to a room to give it an aesthetic value. Throw in one or two well-selected accessories or decorations such as wall art, mirrors, candles, picture frames and rugs. Work with variety but try to maintain balance even as you work this into your space.

5.   **Keep it simple**
The beauty of minimalism is in its simplicity. Adopt the 'less is more' approach to your interior ddcor. Continue to keep space in mind as you work. Your space doesn't have to be boring. In fact, minimalist decorations when done well can be far more beautiful than hordes of decorations staring at you from every corner. Just take it one step at a time and make sure to be fully committed to minimalist aesthetics.

CHAPTER SEVEN - DIGITAL DECLUTTERING

Since the world went digital, our lives have become more comfortable, we have become more productive, and information dissemination is now faster. But there is a downside: we have also become obsessed with electronics and digital devices. The devotion we show these little gadgets has reached an alarming stage. Things that were produced for us to control have now gradually become our masters.

Here is a quick picture: hours on social media, hundreds of unread emails in our inboxes, a desktop littered with folders and files, storage devices filled with hundreds or even thousands of photos, music, and videos. It is overwhelming, to say the least. We never knew it would happen until digital clutter became an important topic.

Since we spend most of our time in the digital world, doesn't it make sense to keep our digital lives decluttered as well? Doesn't it make sense to keep our devices, which make our lives so much easier, as smooth-functioning as possible? How much of the things (documents, files, and folders) saved up in your digital space do you actually need? When did you last do a cleanup of your phone or computer?

Apart from the clutter on our digital devices, there is also clutter that can form from our overdependence on these devices. We spend hours plugged into these gadgets that they now define our happy and sad moments. Shut down your computer or phone and do something more physically or mentally demanding. Even if you work from a laptop most of the time, set out at least one hour per day to do something different like reading a book, taking a walk, talking to another human or even talking to yourself. Live in the real world, not just the digital world.

The Principles of Digital Minimalism

- **Your devices should make your life easier not harder**

That's why they were invented in the first place, after all. Our phone and our computer should be helping our lives function more smoothly, with more ease. They should be helping us navigate obstacles, not creating more. You're not living by this principle if you find huge chunks of your time taken up by your device. Consider if the time you spend on your device is more than the time saved through its functional features.

- **Usage of your device should be intentional not addictive**

How often do you pick up your phone out of habit and anxiety, and not because you mean to carry out a specific action? There's a difference between opening your device to send an email and opening your device because you need to do something, anything, with your hands. Try to only use your device if there is something very specific you need it for.

- **Always put people before machines**

This one should be a given, but it's not, to so many people. We always think we're connecting with people because we're talking to them on the internet; while that's true sometimes, we also tend to ignore the people that are right in front of us to do this. Is your addiction to your phone getting in the way of your everyday interactions? How many times do you find yourself scrolling while you're in the company of someone who is trying to talk to you? Never let your machines take over.

Important Advice for Defeating Digital Clutter

1. **E-mails**: A cluttered inbox is enough to overwhelm you, when all you're trying to do is check up on your latest messages. The problem worsens when you have multiple emails for different purposes. If that is the case, then take it one email at a time.

First, go through the different categories (your inbox, outbox, drafts, sent mail, etc.) and delete everything you do not need a record of. It is a tedious job, but it is worth it. You will find mail that has been there for years and mail that you replied to a long time ago. Work on your contact lists. Which services send you the most emails and why? Do you find the emails helpful in any way or do they just drive you to purchase things you don't need? If this adds to clutter, then unsubscribe, block, or delete.

Adopt a new habit of checking through your mail once in the morning and once in the evening, instead of doing so at random intervals. This way, digital clutter doesn't build up. Declutter your inbox of unnecessary emails every day so that clutter doesn't begin to build up again. Each week, run through your sent emails and delete those that need to be deleted. Cultivate these habits and practices, and make sure you don't fall back into old habits of ignoring digital clutter in your electronic mail.

2. **Social Media:** Social media clutter can manifest itself in a variety of ways. First, there is an accumulation of unnecessary friends and people on your 'following' list. Sometimes you go online and see posts from people that you barely remember how you met. Sometimes you may feel this blanket of guilt coming over you as you unfriend or delete some contacts, but there is no good reason for this. This is a healthy habit for your digital life. There is no need to keep in contact with someone you barely know, especially if what they post is annoying or irrelevant to your life. Delete them and don't feel bad,

Cleaning up your social media accounts on various platforms will help set your priorities straight and feed you with relevant information, pictures, and status updates that you actually care about. Your mind also benefits from this because it will have lesser visual clutter to deal with, and it can focus on what you like.

The same method can be applied across all social media platforms. Streamline all your subscriptions and follow the necessary pages. Connect your accounts across platforms to make your internet experience flow with ease.

Lastly, don't get consumed by social media. These platforms, even with all their numerous benefits, eat your time up. Don't spend more than ten minutes at a time on each platform. Do what you have come to do and leave. You are only allowed to spend more time than normal if you are running a Twitter advocacy group or making money from running Facebook ads. If it doesn't benefit you emotionally, mentally, or financially then you have no reason to spend more than an hour per day scrolling through an app.

3. **YOUR COMPUTER OR LAPTOP**

Most computer systems are digital junkyards. Is yours one of those? Only you can answer. The decluttering process starts by cleaning up your desktop. Think about your desktop as your parking lot or driveway. It is an introduction to your digital home. In fact, by merely looking at the level of organization on some desktops, I can tell how organized the owners are. There are many desktop icons that you don't use. Delete them: shortcuts, folders, and files. If there are documents that you still feel will be important to you in the future, you have the option of backing it up on cloud storage. But be careful, so your cloud storage doesn't suffer from clutter transfer. Only back up the files that you will definitely need in the future.

Keep all icons arranged at the left side of the desktop and ensure that they don't take up more than three rows at a time. If there are files that you reopen occasionally, put them in a folder and name them. Sort everything on your desktop by type.

Next, uninstall any programs that you rarely use. Free up space on your hard drive so your system can operate smoothly. Ensure that every single application installed on your system is one that is used frequently, not just eating space for no reason.

Focus on categorizing your documents into relevant folders so that it will be easier to find each of them when they are needed. You will need concentration for this one and perhaps a pen and book to jot down the name of each new folder and the files in them. With your documents neatly organized in your computer, it will be easier for you to navigate through your system. The goal is to get through each folder and get rid of the excess and unnecessary documents.

Maintain the decluttered state of your computer by constantly deleting unnecessary files you don't need. Become a gatekeeper and keep track of all downloaded files. Keep them organized in the download folder so they can be deleted easily when the time comes.

CHAPTER EIGHT - PERFECTING THE MINIMALISM EXPERIENCE

Minimalism is not just a lifestyle; it is an experience. Everything that we do contributes to the overall journey. These are the experiences that you should seek out, the experiences you should spend your money when you're not spending on useless stuff. Possessions and property gratify the body while worthy experiences delight the soul and mind. The nourishment of the soul and mind is important for the wellbeing of the body. That is why it is impossible to be attracted to an insane person, no matter how beautiful their bodies look.

Stocking our lives and homes with the latest gadgets seems satisfying because it provides you with the thrill of a brand new purchase, but this only lasts for a short period. The thrill dies off, and you are left in the same place you once found yourself: searching for another item to give you the same thrill. The cycle goes on, and you're never more satisfied than you were before. There are better ways for you to spend your money.

Why We Need Experiences More Than Material Things
Money spent on experience is money spent nurturing the soul. The joy gotten from experiences lasts longer than the fleeting joy from purchasing stuff. This is why:

   a. **Experiences help to solidify your own purpose and passions**

Everything that you do and spend money on should influence your future and propel you towards your purpose and passions in life; material possessions rarely compel you to do this. If you're obsessed with mountaineering, owning a hundred books on the topic or a dozen mountaineering outfits can never be equated to actually going on a mountaineering expedition. Material possessions will only fuel your imagination in regards to the experience, but the experience is what actually fuels your soul and satisfies you. This is why people go on road trips to see the country for themselves, not through pictures. This is why people go to music festivals; to see their favorite artists perform in person and not just listen to the same old recording.

b. Shared experiences can foster relationships

An experience shared is a part of you shared. It's as simple as that. It is a bond that remains as long as both parties are alive. Have you ever caught yourself just smiling because the memory of a shared experience has come to your mind? It is a wonderful feeling, isnt it? Experiences shared with people made them closer to you. Think about all the close friendships you have and try to figure out what makes the friendship strong. The chances are high that those friendships blossomed over time because of a powerful shared experience or a series of shared experiences. Once you meet up with people you have shared your experiences with, there is never a dull moment. There are plenty of memories shared between the two parties, and conversations can last hours.

c. Experiences introduce you to new things

A life without new experiences is a boring life devoid of learning and expansion of the mind Experiences can teach you the importance of life and friendship, and they can give you a changed, brand new perspective on the world. Everyone who has ever experienced real and transformative change did so because of one singular experience. Everyday people are discovering their purpose in life because of experiences, something they would have never known if they had chased possessions instead.

d. Craving experiences will eliminate worries associated with buying stuff

In an earlier chapter, we established the degree of anxiety and worry that comes with purchasing new stuff. What if I was ripped off?

What if I get robbed? What if this iPhone I bought for $999 suddenly drops into a bucket of water? The 'what ifs' are numerous and they make you paranoid. It takes up so much mental energy that you become stressed. That is not to say that you should never buy new things and spoil yourself once in a while, but seeking out experiences will greatly reduce these worries. Once you have some money saved up and have gotten your supplies ready, you can make plans and go after any experiences without worry. Your experience can never be taken away from you. Once you get it, it is yours forever, unlike all your material possessions.

Experiences that are Better Than Any Material Object You Can Buy

1. Travel

How long have you remained in the current city or town you live in? A lot of people are comfortable staying in one place for more than a decade without crossing the borders. Just because your place of worship, a shopping mall, school, library and possibly a cinema are available where you reside doesn't mean there's no reason to venture out. Social media has made this situation worse since you can stay in your room and feel like you've traveled across the world through the internet. But there is more to the world than the city you live in. Go out and see for yourself. Don't depend on the pictures.

The feeling of being in a different country, experiencing their culture, and learning their stories is unparalleled. You can eat their local cuisine and learn a new language. You can even travel to the next city and take pictures of beautiful sights on your way there. Visit a relative and spend the night with them. Store the memories from your journeys and expand your mind. You need not travel far; just travel somewhere.

2. Festivals

Festivals bring passionate and excited people from everywhere to engage in a shared experience. Going to festivals with your friends is a great way to bond and meet new people. Even if you get lost and wander to the other side of the festival grounds, there is always a new experience waiting for you. Most of the people that go to festivals are people that share the same passions as you and meeting them will ignite your passion with even brighter flames.

Festivals are filled with culture, life, music, art, and people. There is always something to captivate you, no matter your interests are. Festivals are events where you can be yourself and express your individuality, no matter how weird. There are so many kinds of festivals you can enjoy. Music festivals are by far the most common, but there are also literary festivals and cultural festivals. Try them all!

3. A Weekend Getaway with Friends

You can plan this. All you need to do is to pick a location and travel there with friends. The main thing here is not the destination, but the journey itself. Arriving at your intended location will be fun too, but there's also nothing like getting together with friends and the laughter you share along the way. You don't even have to spend the night, wherever it is you travel to. You can go there in the morning, spend some time and be back by dinnertime.

For example, if you have friends who are art enthusiasts, you can plan to go to a museum or an art exhibition. Savor your experience by allowing yourself to be fully engaged in the program at hand. Or you could go on a hiking trip with friends and you could even camp out in the woods, if you're the outdoorsy type.

The beauty of going on such trips is the uncertainty that awaits you. You never know who or what you will meet, the humor you will find, or the stories that will be shared and created. These are the experiences from which life is truly made. One day, when you think back on your life, this is what you will remember.

4. Learn something new and exciting

The process of introducing your mind to something new will enhance the quality of your life and refine your mind. Your confidence levels will see a boost once you have success with your learning process. As we get older, our minds weaken because we no longer approach new activities or challenges with the same zest of our younger years. This is because we feel more tired and less motivated, not because we are less capable. The mind is always in search of new things to delve deeply into. If you keep on feeding it with routine or the same old information you already know, it keeps on getting weaker and loses its ability to stretch outwards.

It is also incredibly fun to learn new things. Don't see it as an activity you are 'bad' at, but an activity that you can learn from, that can show you a whole new side of the world. So many possibilities open up to you when you decide to grab the bull by the horns and learn something exciting. The process of discovery is filled with so much excitement. It can also be unexpectedly rewarding; you may find that your newfound skills open doors to a promotion or a new vocation entirely.

The Experiences that Make Far Better Gifts than 'Stuff'

We're so attached to the expectation of showing up with a material object in hand, wrapped and ribbon-tied, ready to be opened. The world has fed us the idea that this is what we need to do to celebrate someone. We need a physical representation of our joy, our celebratory spirit. It's time to change this approach. There are many experiences we can gift our loved ones that are far more fun or special than a material object. They may even like it a lot more. Think of the clutter in your home, that heap of stuff that consists of bad gifts that you can't throw away. Don't add to someone else's clutter pile! Consider gifting these experiences:

1. Cooking Classes

Not only do cooking classes teach you valuable skills, they are also incredibly fun! Cooking without having to clean up afterwards? Yes, please! There are classes that teach a range of different cuisines. For something fun, baking desserts is always a great choice. Look online to find classes in your area.

2. A Spa Day or In-Home Massage

Why get someone a bottle of lotion or fragrant oil when you can buy them the experience of someone actually using it on them? It's a far better gift, if you ask me. Purchase a gift card for a local spa or arrange to have a masseuse come to their house. Everyone loves to feel pampered.

3. A Concert Ticket

Whoever it is you're buying a gift for definitely has a favorite musician or artist. See if this singer or band is on tour in the state any time soon. Oftentimes people miss this opportunity because they never think to check if their favorite artist is on tour. Even if they're absolute favorite will not be playing, something similar will also be enjoyable.

4. A Restaurant Gift Card

Many fabulous restaurants offer gift cards for this exact purpose. Treat someone you know to a fantastic dinner. Everyone enjoys a fantastic meal, especially when they aren't paying for it. This gift will not create clutter and it will fill their bellies.

5. Tickets to a Play or Musical

What's wonderful about this gift is that everyone enjoys theatre, but people will rarely buy themselves tickets to a performance. Yet once you're there, you get swept up in what an enthralling experience it is. You always enjoy it more than you think you will. Gift someone this experience because they are bound to have a great time.

6. Yoga Classes

Many yoga studios or instructors will offer a set number of classes for a discounted price. Consider treating someone you know to body-nourishing yoga, especially if you think exercise will benefit them. When someone buys us a gift, we feel like we have to make good use of it or they'll bad. Take advantage of this for something that will truly benefit your friend or relative!

7. Rosetta Stone

One of the best ways to learn a new language is with the program Rosetta Stone. If you know your friend or relative has a fascinating with a particular culture or country, gift them the experience of learning the language of that place. People rarely think to do this, but once they are given the opportunity, they are grateful for it.

8. Membership Programs

This may sound vague, but that's only because of just how much there is to choose from. When you gift someone a membership program, you are expanding their lifestyle. Get them a gym or museum membership. Or perhaps, a yearly pass to their favorite national park or amusement park. Most of these places allow you to buy a yearly pass. One thing is for sure: everyone will love this gift.

9. Free Babysitting

Do you know someone with kids they desperately need a break from? Offer them free babysitting sessions. You could write this out on a card or piece of paper and make it look like an official ticket. Commit to any number of sessions that you think you can handle, e.g. two or three sessions will help a lot but will also prevent you from becoming overwhelmed. It's an unconventional gift but any tired parent will deeply appreciate this.

1 . A Staycation

Why not?! If you know someone who needs to take time out to unwind and feel pampered, pay for a night at a local hotel. Ideally, it should be somewhere comfortable and beautiful. It should be somewhere they'll enjoy more than home. When we get out of our space, we feel more relaxed. I know for sure that one of your friends needs this. Consider gifting a staycation experience!

CONCLUSION

Congratulations on finishing this book! I know the ideas and information I've presented to you have inspired you to begin the decluttering process of your home. The message of minimalism is not preached often, but it should be. Wouldn't you agree? We live in a consumerist world, and some people even frown upon minimalism; don't allow their attitudes to influence you. Protect your minimalist mindset at all costs. Do not allow the things you have learned throughout this book to slip your mind. Once you finish this book, you may even come across an ad telling you to buy a new product right now. Before you consider making this purchase, remember these companies don't really care about you. They just want to sell their product, and they'll tell you anything to make that happen. You are the cow they are trying to milk.

The journey of minimalism is never an easy one. You will come across people who loathe or even despise you for living by a different philosophy. They do so out of their own ignorance. And there is little you can do about it, especially when they aren't willing to hear you out. It is only natural. We, humans, are always quick to condemn things we do not understand. People will jump to conclusions and suggest that you aren't materialistic simply because you are unsuccessful. Of course, you and I know that isn't the case. By now, you've come to a complete understanding of how our quality of life is not determined by how much we own. In fact, clutter and excess can get in the way of our emotional, mental, or professional progress - the real things that contribute to our quality of life.

As I said in the preceding chapters, find your tribe, the people that share your minimalist goals with you. In recent years the conversation about minimalism and decluttering has increased exponentially. Join the conversation on social media and fuel your drive. You will need all the encouragement you can get. You will certainly come across people who have struggled with the things you are struggling with now. They will help you out with any questions you may have, especially now that our journey in this book has come to an end.

The benefits of minimalism are numerous, as I have stated before: freedom from clutter, financial security, and above all, peace of mind. This freedom allows you to chase experiences with a deeper meaning and greater relevance to your goals. You will discover yourself for who you truly are and not what you own. Your confidence will see a big boost because you no longer depend on your possessions and property to determine your value.

It is up to you now. We have gone through all of the most important facets of minimalism: the major habits, the principles, decluttering procedures, tips to reduce mental, emotional, and digital declutter, and much more. It is now up to you to keep practicing and building your great minimalist habits until they come naturally to you. Discipline and consistency are the most important factors in practicing minimalism. Never let go of them. Stay alert of clutter monsters and starve them to death before they become a huge menace. I wish you luck on your minimalist journey!

The end   almostt

Reviews are not easy to come by.

As an independent author with a tiny marketing budget, I rely on readers, like you, to leave a short review on Amazon.

Even if it's just a sentence or two!

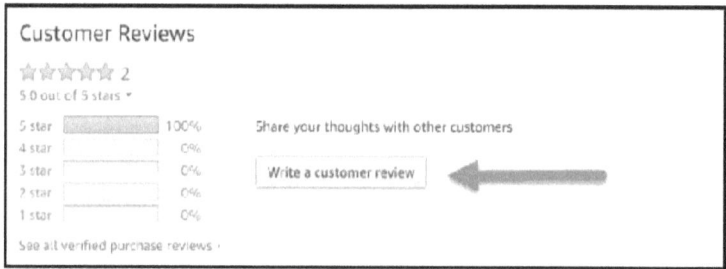

So if you enjoyed the book, please...

>> Click here to leave a brief review on Amazon.

I am very appreciative for your review as it truly makes a difference.

Thank you from the bottom of my heart for purchasing this book and reading it to the end.

www.ingramcontent.com/pod-product-compliance
Lightning Source LLC
Chambersburg PA
CBHW020127130526
44591CB00032B/560